Bribery and Extortion

Bribery and Extortion

Undermining Business, Governments, and Security

Alexandra Addison Wrage

PRAEGER SECURITY INTERNATIONAL
Westport, Connecticut • London

Library of Congress Cataloging-in-Publication Data

Wrage, Alexandra Addison, 1964-
  Bribery and extortion: undermining business, governments, and security/
Alexandra Addison Wrage.
        p.   cm.
  Includes bibliographical references and index.
  ISBN 978-0-275-99649-9 (alk. paper)
  1. Bribery.   2. Extortion.   3. Corruption.   4. International business
enterprises—Corrupt practices.   I. Title.
  HV6301.W73 2007
  364.1'323—dc22   2007020610

British Library Cataloguing in Publication Data is available.

Library of Congress Catalog Card Number: 2007020610
ISBN-13: 978-0-275-99649-9
ISBN-10: 0-275-99649-2

First published in 2007

Praeger Security International, 88 Post Road West, Westport, CT 06881
An imprint of Greenwood Publishing Group, Inc.
www.praeger.com

Printed in the United States of America

The paper used in this book complies with the
Permanent Paper Standard issued by the National
Information Standards Organization (Z39.48-1984).

10   9   8   7   6   5   4   3   2   1

To my husband, Stephen.
Nihil nobis inexsuperabile.

Contents

Preface

This book will take a practical and applied approach to its subject. Although there are several very good academic studies on the history and economic theory of bribery and even some ambitious attempts to isolate and measure its impact, there are no accessible reports on the current practice of bribery. There is no one book to which business-people, employees of nongovernmental organizations, editorial writers, government officials, undergraduates, journalists, and others with a need to know about the mechanics of bribery can turn.

This volume will survey the current practice of bribery. To the extent that it has a message, it is to show that bribery is not a victimless, acceptable, white collar crime whose presence can be adapted to and dealt with lightly. Bribery at all levels, from supposedly "petty" extortion to its grandest forms, is a tentacled crime whose damaging reach is pervasive and nearly incalculable.

For over a dozen years my work has put me in positions where I could observe both bribe-seekers and bribe-payers at close range. Before I studied law at Kings College, Cambridge University, I spent almost two years traveling in China, Southeast Asia, India, and the Middle East. While participating in various volunteer projects, I heard about offi-cials selling their authority to the highest bidder and lost any initial illusions I held about their purely humanitarian motives. When I was injured in China and again when I was sick in India, I saw how under-paid doctors enhanced their incomes by extorting payments from family members of the ill. A few years after leaving Cambridge, I represented a large telecommunications company in the Middle East. While work-ing out of Damascus and commuting across the Bekaa Valley to Beirut,

I received regular lessons in the ways corrupt officials at all levels set up obstacles, from small road blocks to major deal-breaking demands, in order to extract whatever money they could. For four years after that, I was international counsel for a major American aerospace and defense company. In that role, I observed the ways that large corporations deal with their agents abroad and saw how such companies must steer their way through the thickets of the law in countries like Kuwait where one is legally required to work through, and pay handsomely, a local agent, typically one who is related to the ruling family.

Although already interested in anti-bribery compliance, the attacks of September 11 prompted many of us in the field of compliance to question the role that international bribery plays in terrorism more generally. We began to question how countries can keep their citizens safe in the face of corrupt military and police, false documentation, and smuggled munitions, all of which can be bought for so little in so many countries.

These reflections prompted me to look beyond my role as in-house counsel for a multinational corporation. At an anti-bribery conference in Prague in October 2001, I met with my counterparts from other multinational companies and we developed the idea of a nonprofit organization that would support companies in their efforts to comply with the law and to deter the demands of bribe-seekers. That organization, TRACE International, Inc. (TRACE), took shape quickly thereafter. TRACE was established as a membership organization with multinational corporations paying an annual fee. It has prospered in the past five years and now has a substantial philanthropic educational and research arm to complement its original business services branch. My work with TRACE—full-time since 2003—has given me the opportunity to focus exclusively on international bribery, travel and consult widely, provide training in more than fifty countries, and meet with representatives of the governments in Nigeria, India, the Philippines, Yemen, Equatorial Guinea, and elsewhere. I have worked closely with over a hundred companies and several thousand of their representatives overseas. This has been a fascinating seat from which to gather information about the practice of bribery.

Many of the anecdotes recounted in this book were told to me personally. Many others were reported in the media. Of those that were told to me personally, I cannot be certain they are true, but I can say that they were all told to me by people I believe to be credible and by individuals who had nothing to gain from misleading me. What was startling about the research for this book was just how many stories I had to choose from. At anti-bribery workshops in Asia, Africa, and Latin America, as well as those in Europe and North America, even before people learned I was writing a book, they wanted to tell their stories. Perhaps they were willing to talk because bribe-tainted transactions are furtive and isolating and there can be some comfort in passing such stories on. Perhaps it is because people feel they witnessed something remarkable or amusing and they want to share it in a "can you believe it" spirit. Or perhaps it is because they were angered and wanted what they saw more widely known in the hope that sunlight will kill off the mold of corruption. For whatever reason, people passed on their experiences and their behavior has made one thing clear—the days of openly bragging about illicit deals are over.

I have tried to spare the reader any sermons. In fact, I have tried to introduce a little levity in an otherwise grim topic by highlighting some of the most absurd bribery schemes. I know well that this topic is serious and that its impact on people can be devastating, but I hope that I will be forgiven for keeping the tone of this book relatively light-hearted in spite of the subject matter. If I have gone too far for some tastes, I hope readers will still consider the facts and disregard the tone.

Furthermore, I have restricted myself largely to a discussion of public sector (government) bribery, avoiding the wider topic of private sector bribery. I depart from many in the anti-bribery field on this point, particularly with my colleagues in Europe. To be sure, private-to-private bribery is wrong and should be punished. Employees who make decisions about suppliers based on the suppliers' propensity to provide kickbacks should be fired. Executives who sell their corporate decision-making integrity should be terminated and board members removed, but anti-bribery enforcement resources are scarce and many companies have sanctions for abuses of this kind. International anti-bribery laws, on the other hand, serve to protect the interests of citizens who might not otherwise have any recourse against self-enriching politicians and bureaucrats.

Some countries are represented disproportionately in the anecdotes in this book. This is not necessarily an indication that these countries have higher levels of bribery than others. India, for example, has daily news reports of bribery scandals. India may not be more corrupt than its neighbors. It may be that India merely has a freer press. Public discourse about bribery often leads to increased enforcement as government officials see that taking the subject seriously will help them gain a positive reputation and win favor with voters. In countries without a democratic tradition and those with a captive press corps, stories about bribery rarely make the news. In this respect, countries with a tradition of investigative reporting and at least modest free speech are disproportionately represented by bribery accounts in the media.

I would not have set out to write this book if I had not been confident that my husband Stephen, the writer and intellectual in our family, would agree to read and improve every page. Stephen has listened to all of these stories more than once, lived many of them on our travels, and has now read them all repeatedly, too. It delights me to know that in this, as in all things, we have worked together.

I am tremendously grateful to Kerry Mandernach, who patiently edited early drafts, tracked down references, and brought her keen and skeptical mind to every aspect of the book. I also sincerely thank Michelle Gavin, whose help with the chapter on government and whose phenomenal knowledge of Africa were indispensable. Several friends and colleagues read all or parts of the manuscript. I especially appreciate the careful reading, candid comments, and suggestions of Mike Anderson, Ben Atkins, Deb Gramiccioni, Judith Greenwood, and Sue Ringler.

The anti-bribery community has some colorful personalities with whom I have enjoyed provocative conversations over the years. These people, working in corporations, law firms, accounting firms, and government have made the field far more interesting—Fubara Anga, George Brown, Peter Clark, Rich Dean, Tim Dickinson, Pascale Dubois, Greg Dunn, Kate Hamann, Bruce Horowitz, Karina Litvack, Tim Martin, Jason Matechak, Jean-Pierre Mean, Mark Mendelsohn, Martín Montes, Homer Moyer, Mary Jane Schirber, Bill Steinman, Kathee Troy, Martin Weinstein and Jane Wexton. I thank them all for their stimulating thoughts and good conversation and in many cases their fine friendship.

I also have benefited from the scholarly work done in this field as reflected in the bibliography and particularly from the contributions of Daniel Kaufmann, Robert Klitgaard, John Noonan, Susan Rose-Ackerman, and Shang-Jin Wei.

Finally, I owe special thanks to my sons and spirited travel companions, Alexander and Nicholas, who know more about international bribery and extortion than any two thirteen-year-olds should.

Introduction

Thieves, Thugs, and Kleptocrats

In the lore of grand-scale international bribery, there is one man who stands apart from the rest. His story illustrates how bribery can corrode good governance and how it can undermine development, permeate all levels of government, and seep across borders. It also demonstrates how bribery triggers a chain reaction of criminality.

The president's official residence in Nigeria is a grand complex called the Aso Rock Villa. Aso Rock is a great igneous formation that dominates the northeast quadrant of the city of Abuja and thrusts abruptly up almost a thousand meters. The presidential villa is backed up against the rock both for the sake of its grand setting and to take advantage of a natural fortification. "Aso," in the Gbagyi language spoken locally, means "victory" and the people are called the "Asokoro," or "people of victory."[1] Their settlement, until the villa was built on its spot, had survived attempts at conquest for as long as memory extends, and the rock had become an object of worship.

According to the priests of the rock, there exists a secret spring which forms a pool deep in the recesses of the rock, and the waters of this spring may only be drunk on the spot. It is a grave act of impiety to carry any away. These waters, the priests teach, have the magical power of making all who drink them frugal and moderate and free from temptation—they liberate their consumers from the impulse of greed.[2]

On the morning of June 5, 1998, Nigerian President Sani Abacha left the villa at Aso Rock to go to the airport and welcome Palestinian leader Yasser Arafat, who was stopping in Nigeria on his way to Morocco, fundraising as he went.[3] As a Moslem leader, Abacha made a great show of his philanthropy to the Palestinian cause. But after an hour at the airport and the usual formal inspection of an honor guard of the Nigerian Army, Abacha abruptly cancelled the scheduled press conference with Arafat, watched him depart, and then hurried back to Aso Rock for an appointment that did not appear on his official schedule for the day.

Back at the villa, the president met privately with three Indian prostitutes.[4] The rendezvous did not end well. He reportedly prepared for their meeting by taking a triple dose of Viagra, and the drug worked as intended by redirecting blood away from less urgently needed organs. At this dose, his heart was apparently deprived of oxygen and he was dead before the women could flee the room. No autopsy was performed. Instead, the body was wrapped in a shroud, hustled to the airport, flown north to Kano, and hastily interred.

Fearful that her community's warm embrace would prove as fickle as her husband's, Mrs. Abacha opted not to test the patience of a country that had watched its natural resources pumped into off-shore accounts during Abacha's five-year tenure. She had felt the abrupt change in the frosty political wind and had seen that her husband was mourned, as Africans say, "with dry cheeks."

Before the formal mourning period was over, the First Lady pulled out her list of countries that harbor the criminally-enriched and ran her finger down it until settling on what she believed would be a sympathetic country in the Middle East.[5] With thirty-four luxury villas[6] to choose from and a complicated international network of extradition laws to evade, choosing a destination could not have been easy. She grabbed what she could and rushed from the palace to the airport.

Scrambling through Kano airport encumbered by a pile of luggage, Maryam Abacha was intercepted by the Nigerian police. They relieved her of the thirty-eight suitcases she had hastily stuffed with cash.[7] She was escorted out of the airport and back to the sprawling three-wing Abacha family compound, where she resides to this day, in the company of her prized peacocks.[8]

Abacha left behind a vast personal fortune when he died. The family struggles to explain how the general, president of his country but a military man all his life, could have amassed so much wealth so quickly. The people of Nigeria have little doubt.[9] The reign of Sani Abacha—aided by the influence of his family and cronies and the complicity of the international business and financial communities— was marked by every aspect of bad governance and malfeasance that flows from promiscuous, bribe-seeking leadership. During his presidency, the country slid even further into poverty, with more than a third of its citizens living in extreme want. The media was stifled and political opponents were imprisoned, executed, or died mysteriously. Confidence in the government plummeted, while cynicism escalated.[10]

The Abacha story raises doubts as to whether bribery should be considered merely a "white collar" crime, only a little more venal than tax evasion. Bribery in the Abacha style is much more than a grand scale misdemeanor. It is a grave and intrusive kind of criminal activity that reaches into every arm of government, taints every aspect of business, and ultimately unbalances the entire system of government and commerce.

When governing becomes as lucrative as it was for Abacha, some cling to power at almost any cost. The alternative—removal from office—carries the risk of investigation by a successor regime keen to establish its legitimacy, distance itself from the previous regime, and "prove" its commitment to transparency.

Some of the front companies run by friends of the late General for the purpose of managing the Abacha fortune were quickly appropriated by these friends and converted into personal companies. One of these was managed by a former minister who ran an oil exporting business for the Abachas. President Abacha had barely been buried before the business partner seized control of the company.[11] A few years later, another colleague and governor of a small state in the Niger Delta, Diepreye Alamieqeseigha, who is believed to have kept millions of dollars from the Nigerian coffers for himself, was arrested in England and charged with laundering over US$3 million. Alamieqeseigha later skipped bail and escaped, carrying a fake passport and disguising himself as a woman.[12]

More recently, Abacha colleague Timothy Olufemi Akanni died in a plane crash and the Nigerian authorities discovered a US$55 million estate—and a second wife. Assets uncovered were far greater than Akanni's legitimate lifelong earnings.[13] A more civic-minded colleague, Security Adviser Ishmael Gwarzo, is said to have returned US$250 million, claiming he had been given the money and instructed to deliver it to African heads of state at a meeting of the Organization of African Unity in order to tip a vote in Nigeria's favor.[14] Once a dictator sets the tone of frantic self-enrichment in a resource-rich country, a train of malfeasance will follow.

Abacha's death sparked an appalling—but captivating—struggle over the spoils of his vast fortune, which continues to unfold. Nigeria's successor regime, eager to demonstrate its commitment to transparency, but recognizing the challenge inherent in locating and seizing assets ferreted away, offered amnesty in exchange for a deal with the Abacha family: the bribe-takers could keep a portion of their haul and the government would end any further inquiry.[15] The government's offer included the dropping of all charges against Abacha's eldest son, Mohammed, including those for the murder of Alhaja Kudirat, the wife of one of Abacha's political opponents. With this settlement offer, which brushed aside all legal recourse against the family, the government sent the message that a skillful plunderer would be able to operate with impunity and established the rule that those able to steal the most would be in the strongest negotiating position. The startling settlement proposal required the Abacha family to refund 80% of what remained of their liquid assets. That is, they could keep all of their real estate and luxury cars and yachts—and 20% of the remaining cash.[16]

In part, the government may have chosen this option to avoid any penetrating investigation into the dealings of other members of the government in power during the Abacha regime, but it also allowed them to avoid wading through the slow and expensive international legal process to recover assets that may never be found. The Abacha family's willingness to fight—and fight aggressively—was manifest in their selection of defense counsel. The family hired the late Johnnie Cochrane of the O.J. Simpson defense "dream team" fame. Cochrane appeared at an April 2000 pre-trial hearing of one family member, but refused to identify for whom he was working.[17] This strategy has forced the people of Nigeria to spend millions of dollars trying to locate and repatriate the money while the family plays a global shell game with it. But the situation actually got worse for the people of Nigeria. Moham-med Abacha, freed from prison presumably as a first good-faith step in the overall settlement, promptly and publicly rejected the agreement. Roaming free again, there is little incentive for him to negotiate when the family holds all the cards and all the money. Time passes now with the Abachas living in secluded comfort as the money slips further from sight.

THE BAD BOYS CLUB

Successful bribe-takers give rise to rings of criminality around themselves as they dig-in, bolster their nefarious influence, bestow bribe-taking opportunities on cronies and family members, and take whatever steps are necessary to counter opposition. The possibility of failure becomes unthinkable, because it brings with it the possibility of investigation and imprisonment by a successor regime. Instead, the frenzy to steal or extort as much as possible grows and the money typically is moved out of the country to ensure access from almost any country on short notice.

A do-it-yourself manual on international kleptocracy would have to feature Abacha's theft of approximately US$4.3 billion in his five years as President of Nigeria.[18] Some estimates are as high as US$5 billion.[19] The more conservative estimate represents more than US$2.5 million dollars stolen or extorted each and every day he was in office. At the rate he was going, Abacha might have broken Haji Mohammad Suharto's record if his heart had held out.[20] Suharto is believed to have stolen as much as US$35 billion while president of Indonesia. Mobuto

Sese Seko stole US$5 billion while Zaire plummeted to the bottom of the poverty charts in Africa. Ferdinand Marcos of the Philippines stole at least that much and many suspect far more. The secrecy surrounding theft of this magnitude is such that estimates are often based on the number of luxury yachts and personal jets in a kleptocrat's private collection.

In the Bad Boys Club of kleptocrats, these are the over-achievers and the fact that their names are widely-recognized reflects not only the scope of their pilferage while in office, but also the temerity with which they looted. Their confidence in their governments' willingness to look the other way was not misplaced. Not one of these men spent any time in jail. None of them even stood trial. The well-shod Imelda Marcos infamously ran for office after the death of her husband.

What they are estimated to have stolen from those they governed totals more than $50 billion, but they are not alone. Thousands of government officials—both senior leaders and low-level bureaucrats—siphon billions of dollars a year from the global economy. They demand bribes in exchange for allocating government resources for everything from scarce medical services and primary education to major military purchases and vast infrastructure projects.

FACES OF BRIBERY

The Abachas are just one of many families that have transmuted governance into a lucrative family business. One can substitute other names—Baby Doc Duvalier, Saddam Hussein—but the story is much the same. A leader not held to account sets no limits on his greed and plunders a society from above, extracting bribes with such rapacity that the country is crippled and stunted in its development.

More typical bribe-takers count their good years in the thousands, not billions, of dollars. Most are supplementing admittedly meager government wages with what they can skim from each transaction. This face of bribery can be seen at other levels of government. Bribes are demanded from parents in China before their children can attend purportedly free schools. Bribery schemes are devised by executives determined to win business at any cost or to knock their competitors out of the running. Most of the stories in this book are about these more ordinary criminals—the government officials who hold and abuse positions of public trust, namely police officers, state hospital staff, tax assessors, customs and immigration officers, and elected and appointed government officials of all kinds. At best, these petty offenders collectively do their part to erode public confidence in government. At their worst, they jeopardize economic stability, distort markets, discourage foreign direct investment, contribute to unrest, and undermine security.

Unquestionably, multinational companies play a significant role in bribery, but far too little is said about the creativity and tenacity of the legions of government officials on the take. They ask for cash, of course, and wire transfers to numbered accounts. They ask for sweetheart deals on real estate. They ask to have women sent to their rooms. They ask for jobs for their children, scholarships for favored nephews, and medical care for ailing wives. They set up shell companies, off-shore accounts, phony charities, trusts in the names of their family members, and committees that they then manage for their own benefit.

The less well-placed individuals demand jewelry and travel expenses to "visit the factory" in the United States, by way of a long-weekend in Disneyland or Las Vegas. They ask for first class air travel that they cash in at the airport for economy tickets, pocketing the difference, or for four-star accommodation that they subsequently share with colleagues. Major multinational companies are hit up for cases of scotch at Chusok, the Korean harvest festival; cash during the Lunar New Year; and goats for Eid, the festival that marks the end of Ramadan.

Businessmen don't speak out about these government officials—from grasping and clumsy to powerful and frightening—because they are the *customer*. Companies won't speak out against them for fear of losing current contracts or jeopardizing future business. They believe they have to "pay to play." Few locals speak out against them because they are complicit, cynical, or terrified. The officials can stroll down a queue of multinationals repeating the same demand and they risk nothing more than the unlikely and short-lived embarrassment of an empty hand.

It's tempting to point with outrage at a badly run corporation. It's more difficult to sustain that outrage across the thousands of demands set forth in flashy restaurants in distant capitals, where private security guards hover over their charges and waiters fawn over the government officials exploiting their public offices for personal gain.

It's easy to blame the locals for the everything-has-a-price *souk* mentality pervasive in some foreign capitals. It's far more difficult to comprehend the furtive and profoundly isolating nature of most of these transactions. Citizens suffer an utter lack of bargaining power when not only their doctors and teachers and petty bureaucrats are corrupt, but so too are the police who investigate, the lawyers who prosecute, and the judges who adjudicate.

On few issues does the understanding of those living in developed countries—whether or not they venture overseas as tourists or businessmen—and the experience of the local resident differ so dramatically. Too little is being done to reduce corruption because the act is often several steps removed from the victim, making it difficult for public outrage to gain traction.

This book is about Sani Abacha's thousands of small-time imitators. It's about the often clumsy schemes by which government officials sell their authority to the highest bidder. It's about the risk and uncertainty that businessmen introduce into every transaction when they believe that bribery is a good strategy or when they simply accept it as unavoidable. It's also about the misery, despair, and violence that radiate out from corrupt individuals with even just a little power. Bribery has a very personal cost: placing a greater burden on the poor than the rich and on the desperate most of all. Bribery also has a global cost: distorting markets, discouraging foreign investment, undermining security, and eroding confidence in elected officials and in the democratic process.

Every act of complicity encourages the corrupt. Every bribe paid, however casually, shapes the expectations of the recipient for all future transactions. Every bribe resisted, on the other hand, is a tiny victory for the individuals involved, for the larger community, for decency, and for the rule of law.

Chapter 1

Dimensions of Bribery

Corruption is a universal problem. What we see is not a singular phenomenon, is not a curiosity, is not individuals having lost their direction. It looks like a system.

—Eva Joly, former French investigating magistrate responsible for the Elf-Aquitaine Oil investigations, acceptance speech for Integrity Award, 2001

WHAT IS IN A WORD?

"Bribe" is a curt and ugly word, yet it was not always so unattractive. Give the word a French pronunciation with an aspirated "r" and a long "e" for the vowel sound, and it begins to sound a little gentler. It is in fact French in origin, and comes from the French spoken in the late medieval period. It is recorded in the late thirteenth century as meaning, disarmingly enough, "a morsel of bread given to beggars." What could be more kindly than to feed the poorest of the poor?

The French verb *briber* meant to beg, and *une bribe* was a charitable act, a small but well intended gift to the less fortunate—something given with no intent to corrupt but, rather, to support and comfort the weak. There was nothing self-interested in passing out "bhreebes" unless it was done perhaps to earn the giver credit in the treasury of merit that might one day win one a place in heaven.

How did the word for kind alms to the hungry turn into the word for illicit payments and extortion? How did a scrap to a beggar turn into "an offer one can't refuse"? Extort, after all, is another sort of word altogether. It, too, sounds curt and ugly, but there is no pretense about its origin. It plainly comes from the same Latin root as "torture," to twist or wring. It means to wring something out of someone, making them suffer.

It likely was a matter of cynical prevarication. The payers and seekers of bribes were made uneasy by what they were doing. They were eager to use another much more favorable word to disguise the true nature of their act, so they seized on almsgiving for their code word. It is good to have verbal cover when what you are doing is unspeakable. So, in an early bit of Orwellian doublespeak, they co-opted the language of charity to disguise abuse of public office for private gain. The use of a sly, concealing word is one more small violation of trust that bribe-payers commit.

From at least the time of Dante, who featured bribe-takers in a half dozen sites in his vision of Hell, people have used soft and flattering words to make their attempts to buy influence or to sway judgment their way sound more respectable than they are. The list of euphemisms for bribe in use today is long: *une douceur*, "a sweetener," the French call a bribe today, or *un petit cadeau*, a little gift. An Italian cop will ask for "something for the weekend," while Spanish and Mexican policemen will take a *mordida*—a little bite. A Nigerian official will ask "won't you smile at me?" A Russian is more likely just to tell you to pay up. For some reason he is much less shy about his intentions.

It is an old insight by moral theorists that the lies we tell reveal our values. We tell a lie to present ourselves as we would like others to perceive us, to make them think we are something other than we are, to seem to ourselves, and to others to be what we would like to be. The same moral theorists say that the first step in claiming truth and achieving rectitude is the clear naming of things—calling a spade a spade. This renders suspect the use of most words that stand in for the word "bribe." "Facilitating payment" comes to mind, though it is one of the more technical, bland and unimaginative phrases. Even "morsel of bread" is better.

WHO IS STEALING WHAT?

Bribery is rarely a simple, isolated solicitation or payment in exchange for goods, services, or influence. Bribery permeates most forms of international criminality and it gives rise, in turn, to additional crimes. Bribe-takers, illicitly enriched, find they need to disguise the source of their new-found wealth and falsify records to protect the position through which they are able to generate the income. These entrepreneurial bribe-takers keep the funds both safe and accessible and continue to seek new sources of revenue.

Because of the web-like nature of bribery, describing the scope of the problem can be quite complicated. Bribe-takers often must pay bribes in order to ensure their own safety and maintain their lucrative position. Some bribe-takers may keep little or none of what they collect, paying off those above them simply to hold on to their jobs. Others may demand a cut of another's bribes in exchange for agreement not to report them. It can be difficult to identify the line between bribery and extortion. At one end, a company offers a government official a payment in exchange for future business. This is a simple example of bribery. At the other end of the scale, a government official demands a bribe and states that he will ensure that company never wins another contract if it doesn't pay. What lies between the two extremes is often known only to those who participate in the exchange. Who raised the possibility of a bribe first? Were threats, if any, credible? Was payment of a bribe a simple and welcome resolution for the company, an unpleasant compromise or the only way to close the deal? If the latter, what patterns have been set for future negotiations with the same official?

If one of Saddam Hussein's cronies in the Ministry of Petroleum Resources in the early 1990s asked for a meeting at a company's Iraqi oil refinery, the company could hardly decline. Imagine, then, that the crony arrives with a motorcade and eight armed guards, all wearing dark sunglasses and quasi-military attire. He makes himself comfortable, looks around and then comments: "nice refinery you've got here— shame if something happened to it." The groundwork is laid for an extortionate demand.

He then proceeds to lay out a plan whereby the company pays the crony handsomely for his thugs' protection. Once this bit of business is behind the parties, the crony relaxes and starts talking about possible business ventures. He can, he claims, ensure the company gets inside information from his ministry on new projects. He can help the company identify other useful people to include in the pay-off. The company's local revenue can double within a year, he promises.

Another example that tosses nepotism into the mix is that of the procurement officer in China who can "guarantee" a company a steady diet of government contracts if the company will agree to retain a company owned by the official's sister for all subcontract work. If the company decides not to work with the sister, it will "never get another government approval for anything."

Focusing on these two examples alone, anti-bribery practitioners could spend a great deal of time debating which parts of the exchanges describe extortion, which constitute bribery, which might be theft, and which embezzlement. Officials like those in the examples do not ask for money outright. Instead, they stage a scene in which the company representatives, attuned to the signals being sent after years of doing business in the region, will know what is expected of them. They introduce a threat before they propose an expensive solution—or they offer the solution first and threaten only after the initial suggestion proves unsuccessful. The threats may be explicit or a company may just find that the staff of a previously accommodating government office suddenly stops returning their calls. The officials always promise that great wealth will flow from the relationship if only the parties can reach an understanding.

If an official never asks for a bribe, can he be accused of extorting one? A company representative, jaded after years in the region, may raise the matter first to demonstrate his business sophistication and knowledge of the local way of doing business. In my experience, this scene is not at all uncommon. In some countries the exchanges are more furtive, but in many they are surprisingly inane: purportedly, sophisticated executives who tuck a twenty dollar bill inside their passports before handing them to security guards at checkpoints or ask police officers if the problem can't be "settled right here with a fine." These same executives may enclose cash in applications for government licenses and even ask health inspectors to "bring the whole family" next time they visit the restaurant.

GOVERNMENT OFFICIALS

Because government officials occupy a position of public trust, their abuse of that trust is arguably more damaging than similar abuses in the private sector. There are relatively few cases of theft, fraud, and poor governance on the scale of the savings and loan failure of the 1980s or Enron in the early 2000s—both of which caused real hardship to employees and taxpayers and delivered a blow to investor confidence more generally. In both of these cases, the U.S. government responded quickly with legislation that reduced the likelihood of similar corporate malfeasance in the future. More typically, shareholders have remedies available to them when corporations behave badly: they can sell their shares, vote out board members, or report the wrongdoers to government enforcement agents. Finally, supervisors within a company can also act; when a company finds that an employee is funneling work to a single contractor in exchange for illicit payments, the company can fire the employee. In many countries, perhaps most, citizens don't have comparable recourse if their government officials are looting with wild abandon. In some countries, even speaking out against it can be dangerous.[1]

The Foreign Corrupt Practices Act—a U.S. anti-bribery law which will be discussed in more detail in the next chapter—criminalizes bribery of foreign government officials. It does not, however, criminalize private-to-private sector bribery. The U.S. government, at least, appears to have made the decision not to prosecute bribery schemes between corporations unless they are accompanied by fraud or accounting violations. Whereas a U.S. company is likely to hesitate before flying government officials to the World Cup at company expense in order, at least nominally, to discuss business, company policy with respect to a private sector customer is likely to be far more lenient. The laws of most other countries do not distinguish between the two. In countries like China, where state and communist party ownership of traditionally private sector industries blur the lines, many anti-bribery compliance practitioners admit to not being able to determine with confidence whether a bribe was made to a government official or to a private citizen. This book will focus primarily on bribery of government officials. Although all bribes distort free market principles and enrich someone inappropriately, the abuse of trust by those paid to advance the public interest is particularly egregious and will be the primary theme of this book. Some of the examples of criminal activity will include purely private sector players. An executive who pays bribes to win business from private sector customers seems unlikely to live by a different code when dealing with government customers.

SELF-DEALING

Much of this book is about the different forms that bribes can take. The benefits conveyed are varied and do not require that the advantage the official gains be financial or even tangible.

One method by which government officials can ensure that benefits flow in their direction is simple self-dealing. If the official owns shares in a company and directs contracts to the company because of his interest in it, he is self-dealing. If he directs contracts to the company after inflating his company's prices, he probably is self-dealing and embezzling. If he encourages government contractors to buy from his company, he is negotiating a bribe and, if he threatens those that refuse to buy from his company, he is guilty of extortion.

A fairly benign example of abuse of office or self-dealing is the inappropriate use of government property. Government officials in many countries are entitled to use certain government property—cars, *dachas* or vacation homes, private jets, and expense accounts—for official purposes only. If the official uses the jet for prohibited personal purposes, to attend a favorite sports event, for example, he has embezzled the value of the use of the jet and has enriched himself inappropriately. If he actually accepts money from a third party for that party's use of the jet or vacation home, the self-enrichment and impropriety become more clear. This is conversion, a form of theft.

A more common form of self-dealing involves the third party commercial intermediary that isn't what it seems to be. Many companies go to market through third party sales agents, consultants, or distributors. These individuals or, more typically, partnerships or small companies, sell on behalf of their principals in exchange for a commission or similar success-fee structure. When the relationship is kept at arm's length, it is a reasonable way for companies to break into new markets armed with local expertise without the expense or risk of establishing a local office and workforce. Problems arise, however, when government officials have an ownership interest in these commercial intermediaries. If a government official owns the entity that is marketing for a major multinational in exchange for a 15 percent commission, each time the official awards business to that multinational, he guarantees himself 15 percent of the sale. The multinational company may not even be aware of the connection, but is nevertheless complicit in a bribery scheme: paying something of value to a government official, indirectly, in order to obtain business. Companies with robust anti-bribery programs spend vast amounts to vet their commercial intermediaries in an attempt to guard against this very possibility. The laws of most countries will hold them responsible if they either knew or, after reasonable inquiry, should have known about the scheme, but the use of shell companies and blind trusts can obscure ownership from all but the most tenacious investigators.

A more ostentatious example, Abacha was famously adept at all manner of misappropriation. Among the impediments to recovering the money he looted are the complicated and varied schemes he used to steal from his countrymen. Abacha's wealth was reportedly a result of embezzlement, kickbacks to family-owned and shell companies, bribes, and extortion. According to Swiss Judge Daniel Dumartheray, who is investigating Abacha's finances, Abacha "stole money directly from the state, and he used fraud, substantially raising the prices of contracts and getting paybacks, and he got bribes from people who paid to get contracts."[2] Abacha had his hand directly in the till, but this was not his only source of illicit enrichment.

Chapter 6 will cover a similar strategy raised to an art form by Saddam Hussein. Hussein not only plundered his country's coffers directly, but during the period of United Nations sanctions he also orchestrated and rigorously administered schemes by which he was able to steal directly, mandate kickbacks to himself, and extract and extort bribes from those who would do business with Iraq.

EMBEZZLEMENT

Employees, whether they are in the public or the private sector, embezzle when they illegally take for themselves goods or money available to them because of their position. They use their access directly for self-enrichment, misusing their position for personal gain. A bookkeeper who signs checks for fictitious expenses and then cashes them himself is embezzling from his employer. The same is true for an employee who submits fraudulent invoices or inflated travel expenses.

Embezzlement is probably the most direct path to wealth for a government official. The almost ten tons of gold ingots—US$160 millions' worth—that former dictator Augusto Pinochet squirreled away in a bank in Hong Kong were almost certainly embezzled directly from the Chilean treasury during his seventeen-year rule.[3]

According to Enrico Monfrini, a Swiss lawyer representing the Nigerian government in its efforts to recover money embezzled by Abacha, at least some of the Abacha fortune was stolen directly: "We know many of the ways Abacha stole money, including having boxes of cash containing $40 million to $60 million delivered to the presidential villa."[4] Of course, in Abacha's case, no single definition is broad enough to fit all of his many financial crimes.

It should be noted that embezzlement is easier to identify in some countries than in others. In absolute monarchies like Saudi Arabia and the Sultanate of Brunei,[5] it's difficult to know whether it's possible for government officials to embezzle. These oil-rich countries are both family-owned and owe nothing, constitutionally or legally, to their citizens.

BRIBES AND KICKBACKS

A bribe is something of value that passes between two parties to induce the bribe-taker to use his position inappropriately to the advantage of the bribe-payer. "Inappropriately," in this context, masks a world of mischief. Chapter 3 will address the dilemma of gift giving and hospitality. Presumably, when companies wine and dine senior decision makers, it is their intention to persuade them to use their position and influence to the company's advantage—but not *inappropriately*. The boundaries are neither clear nor, for those keen to stay out of trouble, satisfying.

Kickbacks are a form of bribes. While the term "kickback" may simply be used as slang for bribes, it implies a structured arrangement. Kickbacks are illegal commissions; they are bribes on a payment plan— bribes payable only upon delivery of the negotiated *quid pro quo*. For a time, Suharto was referred to in the business community as "Mr. Twenty-Five Percent," because companies operating in Indonesia knew that was the cut that he would demand of each transaction. The terms of kickbacks are clear at the outset of the transaction; a kickback is a negotiated bribe and involves collusion between the parties. The more business a government official sends the bribe-payer's way, the greater his kickback.

Bribes more generally may be spontaneous. They may be made over time, but may also be a single lump-sum. They may be negotiated, or they may simply be an envelope of cash slid across a desk. A bribe can be unsuccessful. The government official can slip the envelope into his pocket without ever using his influence—without even intending to use his influence—to the bribe-payer's advantage. Indeed, it is surprising that this doesn't happen more often as the bribe-payer has no recourse if the bribe-taker reneges on the deal.

If the owner of a construction company wants to win a government contract, he may approach the government procurement officer and offer him a cash bribe to throw the business his way. Alternatively, he may offer to order excess materials to ensure he has enough left over after the project to stop by the official's house and build him a new porch. The latter is probably a kickback insofar as delivery depends on winning the deal, but it is a bribe too. Either way, the government official is misusing his position for personal gain.

When a government official offers a construction contract to a company on a no-bid basis or for an inflated price on the understanding that the construction company will build a new porch on his house as part of the deal, he has stolen from his employer the difference in price and quality between what would have been the most competitive bid and the porch-building winner's bid. Or, at least, he has stolen the government's right to that competitive process. That isn't as theoretical as it sounds. The employer has lost the contractor's incentive to work well and efficiently because the contract is no longer based on competition; it is no longer a contract for the best product or service at the best price. How willing will the tainted government official be to exercise contractual rights to withhold payment or cancel the contract if things go badly? The collusion of the employee has, as is so often said of bribery more generally, skewed free market principles.

In the absence of bribes, customers will make a decision weighing the quality of the products available and the price of each. Typically, within an acceptable range of quality, a customer will buy at the lowest price. Bribes can distort this process wildly. If customers have a side deal that enriches them for selecting one product over another and if, as is the case with government officials, the money to purchase the product isn't theirs, temptation is great to pay more than market price for the bribe-payers product. There are other possible manifestations of distorted market principles. The customer may accept a product that falls outside of the contract specifications. There are examples of pharmaceutical products sold after their expiration dates in which bribes were suspected. A project to complete a major road in Haiti was so riddled with bribery that in spite of full payment being made, in the end nothing was built except the sign announcing the new road.

Previous definitions of misdeeds have emphasized the role of the recipient; this is a good place to acknowledge the role of companies that initiate these payments. Although companies frequently complain of being extorted, many of the cases discussed in this book illustrate the willingness of some corporate employees to violate anti-bribery laws—and the ingenuity and tenacity with which they do it—in their pursuit of international business.

EXTORTION

Two employees of a British company active in Kazakhstan were traveling there in a company truck.[6] They were stopped by a military officer at one of the ubiquitous checkpoints and asked for their paperwork. Predictably, "irregularities" in the paperwork were identified and the employees were asked for US$50 each. Both employees resisted the demand. The officer then shifted his gun, previously strapped over his back, until it pointed at them and gestured for them to get out of their truck. They complied and he began marching them off the road toward a small, metal hut about thirty feet away. At this point, the employees exchanged a look of agreement and suggested to the officer that a fine was probably appropriate under the circumstances. They paid and were permitted to continue on their way. Their payment bought the employees no commercial advantage. This is simple, thuggish extortion. The employees paid the money because they were threatened and believed the alternative to be injury or death.

Purely commercial extortion, where the hostage taken is a business interest, is less compelling, but can wreak havoc with principles of good corporate governance. In one case, a company required heavy equipment to be moved to a construction site for a time-sensitive contract.[7] No government permits or licenses were required; it should have been a straightforward delivery of critical, but not particularly rare equipment. The company was losing tens of thousands of dollars each day that its crew waited for the missing equipment. In this circumstance, no government action was required, but a powerful and opportunistic local official saw the potential in the situation and put pressure on the equipment delivery company to delay the delivery. This is another example of extortion. But whereas few would fault the employees being frog-marched to a hut by the side of the road for handing over fifty dollars, allowing one's company to be bullied over the timely delivery of equipment makes some feel uncomfortably complicit. The company nevertheless paid the money in response to actual and ongoing harm to its business interests. It is worth noting that, in this particular case, the company being extorted was in a joint venture with the local government to which it shrewdly sent a bill for half of the extortionate payment. Future deliveries were not delayed.

Another company recounted the following dilemma in which the company had bid on a large infrastructure project in Argentina in 2002.[8] A company representative knew from the first round of bidding that they had the product with the highest technical rating. Their product was, in short, superior to that of the competitor. When the final bids were opened, the company learned that it also had the most competitive price. The government procurement officer surprised everyone by asking for a two-day adjournment to consider the matter before making a final decision. The senior representative of the company was called in by the procurement officer the next day and was told: "I believe it is in my country's best interests to work with your company, but I want to know how you are going to make me feel good about this decision."

During that and a subsequent discussion, the government official made it clear that he had done a good and patriotic thing for his country by reaching this decision. He also made it clear that he expected a significant payment but that, because it wouldn't alter his good judgment and clear thinking, it was harmless. Interestingly, he seemed keen to avoid appearing to abuse his office, while simultaneously discussing the bribe he expected. In this situation, the company had won the bid fairly on both price and quality. What would happen if the company refused to pay was unclear, especially in light of the very public bidding process that the competitors had just completed. Presumably, some flaw would be identified in the winner's product or some delay introduced. Perhaps licenses to import the product would be denied or payment would be withheld after delivery. The extortionate quality of this demand was clear, but unlike the employees marched at gunpoint or the company awaiting its equipment in the middle of a construction contract, there was less urgency and the cost of nonpayment was vague.

The punch line, in this case, is discouraging. The company declined to make the payment and the project was cancelled without explanation. It was a contract that the country sorely needed and that would, over time, generate significant income. Six years later, the project remains on hold. The official, it would appear, preferred to enrich himself while nevertheless making the best decision for his country, but was both powerful and spiteful enough to ensure that there would be no winners—that no one would feel good about the decision—if his demands weren't met.

FRAUD AND MONEY-LAUNDERING

Bribery schemes almost always include fraud: both deliberate misrepresentation on books and records and concealment of the original source of illegal income. In the first instance, bribe-payers can hardly be expected to enter bribes as such in their corporate ledgers. Instead, bribes are typically mischaracterized as consulting fees, translation expenses, computer services—a particular favorite—or commissions. In one situation, a businessman based in Singapore was reportedly taping bundles of cash to his body before boarding flights into China.[9] He was using the cash to pay bribes in China and accounting for the money as "coffee fund." The company finally uncovered the problem when the coffee fund for a regional office of just eight employees rose to US$30,000 per month. Just as Al Capone was finally nabbed for tax evasion, companies that pay bribes usually trip over their books and records violations.

Effective money laundering often depends on a network of contacts across different jurisdictions, preferably with reliably secretive banks. A government official squirreling away his looted cash must disguise the source if he hopes to hold on to it after he is out of office. It is a blow to kleptocrats everywhere that Swiss banks, among others, now recognize bribery as a crime and cooperate, in most cases, in international investigations. Abacha tucked money away in the United Kingdom, France, Germany, Luxembourg, and Liechtenstein, in addition to Switzerland. According to Judge Daniel Dumartheray, Abacha "had the assistance of a lot of different intermediaries in other countries, and all those people helped him open accounts in the name of other companies, so his name doesn't appear."[10] The paper trail can often be followed, but only as part of an extraordinarily expensive and slow legal process. The Abacha heirs, should they choose to, can keep busy working to disguise the funds and keep the pot of gold just out of reach of international investigators.

CORRUPT PRACTICES

Toss in cronyism, nepotism and patronage—favors and opportunities bestowed on friends, family, and supporters without regard to qualifications—and, individually or in combination, these are the core corrupt practices. A corrupt government official may be extorting or negotiating payments for his own benefit. A corrupt procurement system is no longer functioning for its intended purpose. The term is broad and largely unhelpful. It is easier, however, to refer to a corrupt government official than to a payment-extorting, bribe-paying, tax-evading, money-laundering government official. Examples of financial crimes are included throughout this book to illustrate specific abuses, but these crimes and abuses rarely—perhaps never—occur in isolation.

Chapter 2

The High Cost of Small Bribes

. . . the most sophisticated security systems, best structures, and trained and dedicated security personnel are useless if they are undermined from the inside by a simple act of corruption.

—Ronald Noble, Secretary General, Interpol, remarks before the Opening Plenary Session of the 10th International Anti-Corruption Conference, October 8, 2001[1]

TWO CHECHNYAN WOMEN

Officials at the Moscow airport have a reputation for "informality." Rules are less rigid; security is less consistent. Like so much in Russia, convenience can be purchased by those in a hurry.

On August 24, 2004, two women boarded separate planes in Domodedovo, the larger of the two international airports in Moscow. Just minutes after take-off, the women detonated bombs, blowing up both planes and killing a total of ninety passengers.[2] Neither woman held a ticket upon arrival at the airport, after registration had already closed. Both purchased tickets under the table from an airport "scalper" for US$175, of which US$30 went to bribe the Siberian Airlines agent. It remains unclear whether the security guards' failure to search their carry-on luggage, screen the two passengers, and uncover the bombs was a result of incompetence or additional bribes.

The account in a Russian newspaper of the security checks on the two Chechnyan women quotes the Russian Prosecutor General, who states that prior to purchasing their tickets, "police officers spotted [the women], confiscated their passports and handed them over to a police captain responsible for anti-terrorism operations to examine their belongings and check these people for their potential role in terrorist attacks. The captain let them go without any check, and they started to try to obtain tickets in the same buildings."[3] The ticket scalper and the airline agent were later arrested and charges were filed against the airport's counter-terrorism security officer.

Just eight days after the incident at Domodedovo airport, armed Chechnyans traveled through several police checkpoints to seize control of School Number One in the Russian town of Beslan, taking its 1,200 occupants hostage. Three hundred and forty-four of the hostages were ultimately killed—186 of them children. Survivors of the incident told reporters that the terrorists had chided them to "remember, all your officials are mendacious and corrupt—we paid them all."[4] The government has denied findings of bribery at police checkpoints, but one survivor, Ludmila Boyeva, recounted that the terrorists had explained that they had originally intended to target the larger, more distant town of Vladikavkaz, but that they had run out of money to pay off the police.[5] Subsequent inquiry indicated that two of the attackers had been arrested the previous year, but "freed after a 'substantial' payoff to police."[6]

In the aftermath of these two terrorist incidents, with breathtaking understatement, President Vladimir Putin acknowledged that the Russian government has "let corruption affect the judicial and law enforcement sphere."[7]

CRIMINALIZING TRANSNATIONAL BRIBERY

In 1977, the United States became the first country to criminalize the payment of bribes by its citizens and companies to foreign government officials. It was a bold move at the time, and followed a scandal and subsequent inquiry during which a staggering 400 companies stepped forward and admitted to paying hundreds of millions of dollars in bribes overseas.[8] The law was heralded as an important and necessary measure to restore public confidence in the business community.[9]

That law, expanded twice since 1977, is the U.S. Foreign Corrupt Practices Act (FCPA). The FCPA makes it a crime to offer or pay anything of value to a foreign government official,[10] directly or indirectly, to corruptly obtain or retain a business advantage. It is an elegant law on paper, but the absence of clear and practical guidelines has emboldened the enforcement authorities that prosecute and has been a boon to the defense lawyers who defend companies from its vague standards.

The FCPA is expansive in its definitions. Under its provisions, it is a crime simply to offer a bribe, even if it is never paid and even if the official throws you out of his office, outraged. A bribe may be anything of value and needn't be cash. Enforcement actions have described purchases of office furniture,[11] upgrades to first class travel,[12] jewelry,[13] speed boats,[14] gift certificates,[15] expensive wine,[16] political contributions,[17] and contributions to an official's favorite charity[18] as evidence of alleged FCPA violations. A company may be found guilty of bribery if it makes a payment directly, but also if it hires a local representative who makes the payment to advance the company's interests[19]—with or without the company's actual knowledge.[20]

By 1977, many countries had laws prohibiting the bribing of their own government officials, but the ability of the FCPA to reach across borders and grab defendants by their corporate collars was new and remained unique in the world until almost twenty years later, when the world saw the adoption of a parade of new international anti-bribery conventions. Critics argued that the FCPA was just another example of the Americans' desire to police the world and that, in any event, it was unlikely to change the way companies did business internationally. Champions lauded the law as an important first step in introducing a cost to bribery—risk of prosecution—where previously there had been none.

GREASE PAYMENTS

When the FCPA was first enacted, much of the American business community was made nervous by the competitive disadvantage they expected the new law would bring. Members of the business community lobbied the government successfully for an exception for "facilitating payments" to be carved out of the criminal provisions. The law, still valid on the books today, does not prohibit "any facilitating or expediting payment to a foreign official . . . which is to expedite or to secure the performance of a routine governmental action."[21] That is, payments may be made by U.S. companies to encourage a foreign government official to do his job or to do it in a more timely manner. For example, if an employee of a state-owned telephone company in Moscow offers to install your new phone system "early in 2012," you may choose instead to pay him US$50 to get the system up and running that afternoon. He is the telephone installation man; installing phones is his job and is in no way discretionary, but the company's challenge is to ensure that telephone service is secured quickly enough that business is not disrupted needlessly.

Another common example of a situation in which a payment may be made is the unfortunate fruit company that wants to ship its bananas, but faces a customs agent who has calculated that it will take two weeks for every last banana to rot and has indicated that he expects to be able to process the shipment on the fifteenth day. A U.S. company, under these circumstances, is permitted under U.S. law to pay a bribe ("facilitating payment") to the foreign customs official without fear of prosecution back at home. It may be called an incentive, a backhander, a grease payment, baksheesh, or a tip, but it is a bribe. It is an inducement to a government official to use his public office for private gain.[22] These bribes are paid to obtain visas, permits, and licenses; to expedite government-mandated inspections or to process official paperwork; to ensure police protection; to obtain mail delivery; and to encourage timely testing for drivers' licenses or other official qualifications. They are, in short, a second payment to a government official for a service he is already bound to provide under the terms of his employment.

It's worth pointing out the double standard inherent in the U.S. approach. U.S. law permits facilitating payments overseas in recognition of the difficult markets in which U.S. companies operate. U.S. law does not permit these payments within the United States. It would be difficult for most Americans to imagine sidling up to a customs official at the Baltimore port and slipping him US$100 to expedite customs clearance, although this almost certainly happens.

THE TIPPING MYTH

Facilitating payments are often explained away as a humane response to the low wages of the government officials who expect or demand them. "How," some businessmen ask, "can these requests be refused when an official making just $20 or $30 a month asks for a $5 payment that will help him put food on his family's table?" It is often these same businessmen that explain that a more senior bureaucrat will require a larger facilitating payment. If the original logic holds, however, the largest payments should go to the most junior officials in recognition of their more impoverished state. We tip the person who cuts our hair, but we don't tip the owner of the salon because we assume she's doing just fine for herself.

Another argument in favor of the comparison to tipping is that both tips and facilitating payments are made in the hope of receiving a *quid pro quo* in the form of better or faster service. Tipping is based on a typically unspoken agreement between the owner of a restaurant and the customer that the latter will bear some of the cost of the service within a predictable range and the owner can, as a result, pay the wait staff miserably with a clear conscience.[23] Indeed, the tipping phenomenon is so formulaic and widespread in the United States that many restaurants openly include a tip for large parties in the bill without obtaining the parties' consent.

In his extensive treatise on bribery, John T. Noonan emphasizes the employer's consent to the interferences with his employees' independent judgment. The employer agrees to and benefits from the incentive scheme, which is conducted openly. In distinguishing tips from bribes, there are two important additional differences. First, tips lack an extortionate quality. Even those of us who have been tyrannized by surly waiters know that we have recourse short of paying an undeserved tip. The payment follows delivery of the service, so the service cannot be withheld. We can leave a smaller amount or nothing at all, although we're sufficiently well-trained in this custom to cringe at the thought of doing the latter, or we can speak to the restaurant's management if the situation deteriorates. Second, if we do speak to the restaurant's management, we will have confidence that their interests are aligned with ours. That is, the restaurant owner knows there are other restaurants from which we can choose and, in almost every case, the owner will ensure the customer's concerns are addressed. In the few cases in which this doesn't happen, the customer may simply determine never to return. Within reason, a customer can encourage good service and discourage incompetent or slow service by paying larger or smaller tips. By comparison, the nature of expediting or facilitating payments is that there may be only one telephone installation person, one customs official, or one building inspector making up the rules and, typically in countries with widespread bribery, his superiors are often in on the fleecing.

THE CORPORATE TAX ARGUMENT

Another argument in defense of facilitating payments, particularly with respect to developing countries, describes facilitating payments as a form of corporate tax that the country is otherwise too disorganized or chaotic to collect. Under this argument, payments of this kind bear the hallmark of good corporate citizenship in the absence of competent national governance. The company is supplementing the salaries of poorly paid bureaucrats and, by so doing, bearing an appropriate share of the cost of the services upon which it relies. If a company relies on the customs officer or police or building inspector of a developing country, shouldn't the company pay a portion of the expense associated with these services? While providing some comfort to bribe-payers, this argument has three flaws.

First, and this will be discussed in more detail below, these payments are illegal in the country in which they are made. It is condescending for multinational companies to determine that the payments contribute to some vaguely beneficial redistribution of wealth and so are appropriate in spite of local legislation rendering them illegal. If, as is probably the case, American police officers or immigration officials were determined by public consensus to be underpaid, the initial public response would be to encourage a re-evaluation of their compensation, not a manila envelope stuffed with cash under the table. We should not assume that developing countries welcome foreign intervention of this kind—intervention that permits companies to buy the police protection they need and leaves local citizens underserved.

In addition, there is a considerable transactional cost to these payments. If fees were formalized, predictable, and uniform, this argument would carry more weight, but they tend to apply differently to large companies than to small. Small companies complain that they have less clout in-country, including less support from their embassies and, as such, report being susceptible to more aggressive demands.[24] Rates are reported to be much higher for companies in time-sensitive industries.[25] Apart from a handful of West African countries that have been brazen enough to publish quasi-official "fee charts" for facilitating payments, each encounter must be negotiated separately, arrangements for payment must be made—typically in cash—and the transaction results in no certainty, no enforceable agreement, and generates no receipt for purposes of corporate record-keeping. A case discussed previously illustrates the furtive nature of this culture when a young businessman based in Asia tapes wads of cash to his body before flying into China where the money is used to make facilitating payments.[26] These do not seem to be the actions of an archetypal "good corporate citizen."

Finally, when government officials at any level are either encouraged or simply permitted to use their positions, unchecked, to generate revenue, these positions become disproportionately lucrative compared with others in the community and can develop their own internal kickback culture. A driver who worked for a multinational company in Damascus explained that embassy drivers earn more than doctors or lawyers in that country because of the near-constant opportunity for petty abuses of their position.[27] It cannot be good for a community to have its talented youth aspire to the role of middlemen at bribery flashpoints. The driver recounting this was well-educated and fluent in English; he stated that he had applied for a position at the embassy, but that he believed he was unsuccessful because he hadn't paid-off the right people. The theory that companies are helping to pay impoverished government officials whose countries could not otherwise afford to compensate them is undermined further when one considers the natural resources wealth of some of the countries with widespread bribery: Russia, Nigeria, and Mexico, for example, are all countries with high levels of routine bribe demands and all place in the top ten worldwide for oil exports.[28] These countries may lack the political will to compensate their low-level government officials, but they do not lack the resources. An unofficial corporate tax may keep the peace in the short term, but will not resolve the systemic governance problems these countries must eventually face.

FACILITATING DECLINE, DISTORTION, AND DISASTER

The problem is not just that the justifications for tolerating small grease payments are specious; it's that relatively small bribes—what some call "petty corruption"—can lead to profound consequences. Reducing the scale of these facilitating payments is often considered less important or urgent than reducing "grand" commercial bribery, but there are several problems with payments of this kind and they are, in many respects, more corrosive of good governance than larger, more predictable commercial bribes.

It is not lost on those residing outside the United States that the decision not to criminalize these payments in 1977 effectively permits Americans to violate the laws of foreign countries. There have been no cases, as one might imagine, of U.S. companies invoking this exception to bribe government officials in Canada or the United Kingdom. Instead, the exception is invoked with cultural condescension in countries deemed too difficult to navigate without bribes. This exception to the U.S. law provides a veneer of respectability for payments that are nevertheless bribes and contributes to the general understanding of commercial bribery as somehow less egregious than other financial crimes. No country anywhere in the world expressly permits the bribery of its government officials. When a facilitating payment is made, it may not run afoul of U.S. law—and Canada and Australia have similar exceptions to their anti-bribery laws—but it violates the local law. Permitting—or at least expressly declining to prohibit—the citizens of one country to violate the laws of another on the grounds that it is how they do business there, undermines international legal standards. Multinational companies rely on international legal standards for the predictability and enforceability of their contracts and should not undercut these lightly.

Based on the sheer number of companies operating internationally as compared with the number of active enforcement agents, odds are that most companies will not bump up against anti-bribery enforcement authorities. Short of actual indictment and mandatory remedial measures, companies are left to police themselves for good governance and robust internal controls more generally. In this respect, facilitating payments send a very mixed message. It is often difficult to convey to businesspeople that the payment of large bribes is a crime and will subject them to significant sanctions, including large personal fines and possible jail time, but that small, routine bribes of this kind are acceptable. This can confuse people genuinely trying to comply with a network of conflicting legal standards and can embolden those already in search of a loophole.

In addition to their inherent illegality under the laws of the country in which they are paid, facilitating payments can erode the local community's confidence in companies and their commitment to good corporate citizenship. They can undermine the reputation of the company and generate hostility toward the country in which it is headquartered. When companies pay to jump the queue, they're jumping in front of a local business or individual. Facilitating payments erode good governance and invite representatives of multinational companies to determine for themselves when they should abide by local laws, however time-consuming and arduous, and when to simply wave a twenty dollar bill in surrender.

The dignity of a nation's government also suffers when its representatives develop a reputation for petty scams. Citizens of the country in question tire of hearing examples of rip-offs perpetrated by their elected and appointed officials[29] and those of investing countries revert to short-hand descriptions of countries as "dirty" or "corrupt" until the perceived levels of bribery are in danger of displacing the reality on the ground. The more systemic the demands for bribes are, the greater the indictment of the country involved. No government can control every opportunistic bandit in its midst, but steps can be taken to avoid the appearance that the scheme is sanctioned by the state.

If the boundaries of each transaction were easy to identify and effortless to enforce, these often modest bribes to small-time officials would be less worrying, but they are neither. As we saw in the Moscow airport, it is not safe for bribe payers to assume that the money they use to grease the palms of immigration officials, police officers, or cargo inspectors for purely business purposes will be distinguishable to the recipient from similar payments from those with malevolent intentions. Payments of this kind can wear grooves for the convenience of the criminals that follow behind. In the international business world, this is the point at which corporate executives, thugs, and criminals have most in common: the desire for expediency and reduced red tape. It is not true, of course, that the payment of bribes for a purely commercial purpose—to jump to the head of a customs queue—gives rise to the same level of culpability as bribes paid for more wicked purposes. But it is true that the calculations and habits of bribe-payers—to undermine the system and to find and rely on others who will do the same—and the recipients themselves are often the same. German officials report an unsuccessful attempt in November 2006 to smuggle a bomb on to an airplane at the busy Frankfurt International Airport. The prosecutors have stated that the terrorists had found an airport guard willing to accept a bribe in exchange for smuggling the bomb past security checks, but that the parties were still haggling over the amount of the bribe when the plan was uncovered.[30]

Court records, media accounts, and representatives of multinational corporations provide examples of the many schemes government officials develop to skim their imagined "shares" off of each transaction. When these officials are tapping their creative reserves to develop these plans, and when companies cooperate in their abuse of authority, it is unlikely that the full costly and corrosive impact of the activity is visible to the participants.

In addition to undermining the rule of law, confusing those who wish to avoid illegitimate activity, damaging the reputations of both those paying and those soliciting bribes, and creating opportunities for other kinds of criminal activity, facilitating payments carry with them even more hidden costs, each of which is illustrated below. The neediest among us suffer, whole socioeconomic incentive structures are turned on their heads, the cycle becomes self-perpetuating, and the integrity of the most basic functions of the state—providing security and protecting the borders—are auctioned off to the highest bidder.

THE MYTH OF THE VICTIMLESS CRIME: AMERICAN RICE

As discussed above, some still argue that bribes are akin to tipping—that underpaid government officials rely on these "gratuities" to feed their families. It is true that government officials are often underpaid in developing countries, but few would argue that low wages justify freelance criminality. It can be difficult to connect these often small-time interactions to see the larger, corrosive pattern. "Tipping" hints at two myths that need debunking: bribery is not a victimless crime and bribery is rarely just about the two people engaged in the transaction.

Rice is an important part of the Haitian diet and Haiti does not grow enough rice to meet local demand. Beginning in the mid-1990s, American Rice Inc., one of the largest U.S. exporters of rice to Haiti, found itself faced with customs delays and a growing tax burden. Under the management of its president, Douglas Murphy, and the company's Vice President of Caribbean Operations, David Kay, the decision apparently was made to bribe local Haitian officials to reduce the company's customs duties and tax bill.[31] As so often happens with quasi-official tollbooths of this kind, the payments appear to have become a matter of habit over time. Murphy and Kay were not thugs. They were both long-term corporate employees. As one prominent anti-bribery lawyer put it: "these guys are not your typical criminals. If you invited them to your home for dinner, you wouldn't lock-up the good silver."[32] After their payments were uncovered, they fought the indictment, claiming that their actions fell squarely within the FCPA's facilitating payment exception and, at their first trial, the judge agreed.[33] It was only on appeal that the U.S. government prevailed.[34]

During the time that these bribes were paid, the citizens of Haiti paid a triple tax on their imported rice. Although presumably not a line item, the price of the bribes would have been included, ultimately, in the price of the rice, just as legitimate shipping costs are. The American Rice executives also paid Haiti officials to lower duties and taxes on import, which would otherwise have contributed to Haitian coffers. And, throughout these illicit exchanges, the people of Haiti were paying the salaries of the officials who were exploiting their positions to thwart the country's importation laws and to enrich themselves.

Both parties to the bribery scheme had grown comfortable with habits of petty criminality.

It is possible that officials on the take choose their shady business partners with care—that they accept bribes only after assuring themselves that the systems to be circumvented are purely commercial—but it seems unlikely. Rather, growing reliant on the additional income and emboldened by the absence of oversight or sanctions, it seems more likely that officials ask few questions of their benefactors. It is difficult to imagine that the tainted official would react differently when offered a payment to avoid the inspection altogether, pulling back and asserting critical national security issues, as opposed to a situation in which he is paid merely to expedite it.

DISTORTING MORE THAN MARKETS: PYRAMID SCHEMES

There is a strong link between countries with high levels of bureaucracy and those with high levels of bribery.[35] More layers of administration generally mean more opportunities to extort payments. Bribery is rarely a spontaneous or isolated act initiated by renegade officials. Most bribery schemes involve multiple layers of authority, with one or more officials at each level insisting on his cut.

A young police officer in Moscow made an unlucky decision.[36] His second shake down on a miserable winter's evening in early 2003 was an American lawyer who had managed to hold fast to his "zero tolerance" policy throughout his stay in Moscow. The officer asked to see the American's documentation and then began the heavy sighing and feigned disappointment upon finding things "not quite in order." After statements of regret and hand-on-heart gesturing, he suggested that the US$50 fine could be paid directly to the officer, avoiding a trip to the police station and related "unpleasantness." It was all designed for the American's convenience, of course.

The American commented that Russian fines are not typically collected in U.S. currency and went on to explain that he wouldn't be paying the informal fine. "We can go to the station if we really need to, but can't you just call it a night for shakedowns?" The police officer, just nineteen or twenty years old, smiled a bit ruefully and said: "Let me tell you how this works."

The two ended up chatting for almost an hour over a coffee while the story unfolded. Jobs that pay enough to live on are pretty tight in Moscow. Government wages haven't kept pace with the increased cost of living and people are struggling there as they are in many big Russian cities. A job as a police officer is better than most and competition for the positions is heated. Those who secure the slots usually do so because a friend or family member has intervened. From the earliest days on the job, new officers are expected to use their positions to generate revenue and to use that revenue to pay-off the officers above them. The American suggested that the officer opt out of the scheme and, in effect, "go straight," but the officer stated that his supervisor would demand his cut whether the officer collected it or not and that his job would last only as long as the payoffs continued.

Every country has some corrupt police officers and many officers in Moscow may be honest. This sort of payoff scheme is most widespread amongst those government departments that interact with the public: police, customs and immigration, tax officials, even those who issue drivers' permits. The trend, mentioned previously, has even been documented showing a "brain drain" in developing countries from highly-skilled professional positions to jobs with exposure to the public, and especially to the business community. "Talent is misallocated, as the jobs with the potential to collect lucrative graft attract people who otherwise would accept the more modest financial rewards of truly productive occupations."[37] To be a low-level customs official can be far more lucrative in many countries than to be a highly-trained physician. Even the most entrepreneurial surgeon can only extort the life savings from a poor patient. But a customs official can hope to skim an "expediting fee" from every commercial shipment passing through his hands and the market for a police officer in a country under siege from within is limited only by his imagination and the hours of his shift.

The pyramid scheme described by the Russian policeman is characteristic of many markets. The official interacting with the public, and so best able to deliver the demand, must keep those above and around him happy if he's to maintain his position. In one West African country, companies have described published lists of "tips" required to get service from government officials and the value of the tip carefully tracks the seniority of the recipient.[38] This is, at least, transparent extortion.

ASKING FOR TROUBLE: CAIRO AIRPORT

Constant demands for bribes can be exhausting. They can turn bureaucratic hurdles into a scene from a Turkish souk, with haggling and feigned expressions of outrage. The consequence for refusing to pay can be as dire as false imprisonment in gruesome conditions after appearing before equally corrupt judges. On the other hand, payment can lead to more and greater demands once the payer is marked as a willing victim. One worrying trend amongst cynical businessmen is that they are hearing demands for payment when, in fact, none have been made.

Apparently, sophisticated businessmen can actually help to create a market for bribes wherever they go. One very senior executive once patiently explained that it simply isn't possible to make one's way through the Cairo airport without a roll of twenty-dollar bills. As the tens of thousands of tourists and business people who pass through that airport each year can attest, many have no trouble at all and wouldn't recognize the airport that he described. The executive drew dramatic verbal pictures of customs officials and passport inspectors and even airport staff stepping in his path at every turn. These officials, he explained, clucked and sighed apologetically and explained how inefficient things were and how much they wanted to help. There were delays waiting for visas—which can be obtained at the airport on arrival—delays with luggage and delays with customs clearance.

It seemed not to have occurred to this gentleman that the inefficiencies might have been legitimate and the officials' expressions of dismay sincere. Perhaps they were—and perhaps not. It is possible that they were thinly-veiled requests for cash in exchange for making everything move a bit more smoothly. Rather than assume the best of these junior officials, however, the suave businessman assumed they were on the take and that there wasn't any problem in the Cairo airport that couldn't be solved with a twenty-dollar bill. In the end, the assumption becomes self-fulfilling. Any well-dressed businessman strutting through almost any airport in the world with a wad of twenties will find someone willing to take the money off his hands.

There is a possibly apocryphal story that describes a British oil executive anxious to depart West Africa for his home in London. The holidays were just days away and he was keen to be on his way home. An airport official approached the impatient traveler and explained that his flight would be delayed four hours. In response, the executive wearily peeled off a fifty-dollar bill and handed it over. The airport official accepted the bill, stared back a bit blankly, thanked the executive and repeated apologetically that the flight would nevertheless be delayed four hours.

It is possible to be *too* knowing. It is possible to have been hit up for bribes so often and to have become so jaded that you begin to see demands where there are none. Even if the demand is real, few bribe-takers will ask for payment directly. If one resolutely declines to hear their demand, it's often too awkward for them to repeat the request more plainly.

Some international businessmen claim never to have been asked to pay a bribe. This may be true. Few government officials at any level step forward with a blatant demand for a bribe; they expect people to understand it when they hear it. The vocabulary of bribery is creative and varied. In Nigeria, a customs official asks if you are "a good guy" and whether "the sun will shine on all of us?" Many will argue that they don't have enough energy for the hassle that follows a refusal to pay, but the hassle often begins with the acquiescence, not the refusal.

Representatives of multinational companies operating overseas describe a consistent trend. When these companies pay bribes to resolve some short-term nuisance, they report that the bribe-taker returns, the word spreads, and the demands multiply.[39]

Shortly after the first Gulf War began, government security guards at a corporate facility in Qatar demanded a US$50 "tip" to compensate them for the increased risk they perceived as a result of mounting anti-American sentiment in the region. These were employees of the Qatari government; protecting the facility was their job. Leaving aside the broader concern that they might have been equally willing to sell their allegiance to the bad guys for US$75, the demand was extortionate. When the company paid—and they believed they couldn't afford not to—they permanently changed the nature of their relationship with these guards. Soon, the guards were requiring payments for evening meals, unofficial overtime, and small "gifts" of cash on holidays, both Moslem and Christian.

Customs officials demand additional fees for clearing your goods: "in cash, please, and not out here in the lobby—let's step into my office." Tax authorities threaten an audit or an inflated tax bill if demands aren't met: "your permits don't seem to be in order and the facility will have to be closed if this can't be resolved 'just between us'." Each time a businessman responds to a demand with a payment, he paves the way for the creation of new and higher hurdles which he will have to buy his way past.

Entrepreneurial bribe-takers will not waste time on those who resist, those who make a fuss, or those who either sincerely or willfully fail to hear the demand being made of them. They will look instead for those who have shown a willingness to buy their way through these bureaucratic toll booths.

The audacity of bribe-takers is staggering, but it is less surprising than the willingness of businessmen to participate in their own extortion. Do executives want to peel off twenties for every administrative task? No. Do they want to have new obstacles placed in their path that they must then pay to remove? No. Would they prefer to direct their "charitable giving" as they see fit, rather than have it extorted from them when time and business pressures are mounting? Presumably.

Instead of risking an awkward exchange or an administrative inconvenience, people pay up. Thousands of brief, uncomfortable encounters result in the sloughing-off of tens of thousands of dollars to the junior officials that circle around these opportunities. And then, one day, these junior officials are promoted.

MOVING GOODS ACROSS BORDERS

The United States Department of Homeland Security, through U.S. Customs and Border Protection, has responsibility for securing American borders. This protection extends to preventing and detecting the illegal movement of people and the illegal movement of goods. While most officers work diligently to fulfill this mission, and many have died in this dangerous line of duty,[40] bribery has taken a toll on the effectiveness of this bureau. Take U.S. Customs and Border Protection agent Fernando Arango, for example. Arango pleaded guilty in 2006 to letting a motor home pass through Mariposa checkpoint on the Mexican border with Arizona.[41] He accepted a US$50,000 bribe to overlook a 440-pound shipment of cocaine that Arango himself had advised the driver to hide in a false compartment built for that purpose. In another bizarre tale of full-service bribery, three former police officers in the same area were convicted of providing a police escort for vehicles filled with narcotics in exchange for US$1,000 and US$1,500 payments.[42]

From late 2001 to 2004, the Federal Bureau of Investigation ran "Operation Lively Green," which resulted in forty-seven guilty pleas and involved uniformed U.S. military personnel protecting shipments of cocaine while carrying Army I.D., and driving official vehicles, including two military Humvees. They invoked their official status "to prevent police stops, searches, and seizures of the narcotics as they drove the cocaine shipments on highways that passed through checkpoints manned by the U.S. Border Patrol, the Arizona Department of Public Safety, and Nevada law enforcement officers."[43] On one August afternoon in 2002, some of the military personnel met a twin-engine aircraft on a desert airstrip in Arizona and supervised the unloading of 60 kilograms of cocaine into their military vehicles, all while in full army uniform.[44]

The Federal Air Marshals, who also work under the Department of Homeland Security, have played an increasingly important role in American security over the last five years. An undisclosed number of Air Marshals travel undercover on domestic and international flights and are trained to observe suspicious behavior and to diffuse potentially dangerous situations. Two Federal Air Marshals presumably spotted the opportunity in their special status. In April 2006, they were convicted of agreeing to use their critical security positions to bypass airport security and to smuggle cocaine onto flights.[45] Although the flights in this case were domestic, there are comparable opportunities for Federal Air Marshals on international flights. In addition, and as part of the criminal chain reaction that bribery typically triggers, the two marshals were also found guilty of attempting to bribe a third government employee to advance their drug-smuggling scheme.

Government officials enriching themselves through complicity in smuggling schemes is not new or unique. In 2000, China indicted a former military intelligence chief and member of the People's Liberation Army for his alleged role in a vast smuggling operation involving about US$10 billion in smuggled goods.[46] China, a state which takes national security very seriously, must have been startled by the ease with which its borders were undermined. Originally sentenced to death, the official later received a reduced sentence of twenty years in prison.[47]

Although the illegal movement of commercial goods across national borders undermines revenue collection and places legitimate commercial interests at a competitive disadvantage, more worrying is the network that is put in place to support a smuggling operation of this magnitude and the other uses to which it might be put.

MOVING PEOPLE ACROSS BORDERS

For many people, discussions of bribery bring to mind images of a slick businessman seated across from a bloated government official in the darkened back corners of a smoke-filled restaurant. Junior colleagues form an entourage at a respectful distance and waiters hover nervously. The government official exhales a long smoky breath and names his price. The businessman clutches his heart in mock horror—*it isn't his money, after all*—and the banter continues through a bit of gentle and good-natured haggling. The two conclude the deal over drinks and all that remains are the details of offshore accounts and polite comments from each about how they hope to do business again.

While this scene has undoubtedly unfolded in thousands of restaurants, bribe-payers and bribe-takers can be a much more imaginative group than this suggests. For example, in 2000 and 2001,[48] Hydro Kleen Group Inc., an oil field services company based in Alberta, wanted an edge over its primary competitors—Innovative Coke Expulsion (ICE) and Eliminator Pigging Systems. A traditional approach to graft, presumably, would have had them approaching their primary customers in the United States and elsewhere and offering some personal benefit in exchange for business.

In this case, however, the only Canadian company to be prosecuted for transnational bribery developed a perversely inspired plan. According to the Canadian court documents,[49] Hydro Kleen approached Hector Ramirez Garcia, a U.S. Immigration and Naturalization Service inspector, for help. Garcia was stationed at the Calgary International Airport and was in charge of permitting or denying entry into the United States to those hoping to fly there directly from Calgary. In exchange for a total of just C$28,300 (US$24,800), Garcia agreed to expedite approval of work permits for Hydro Kleen employees.

Emboldened, Garcia subsequently took the startling additional step of placing the names of key employees at ICE and Eliminator Pigging Systems on the national automated "immigration lookout system," a list of undesirables from petty criminals to terrorists to whom the United States seeks to deny entry.[50] Hydro Kleen's competitors were unable to get into the United States to meet their contractual obligations and one company was reportedly driven into bankruptcy.[51]

Garcia suffers from the double ignominy of serving jail time for compromising himself for one of the smallest bribes on record and for his willingness to compromise the national security of his country— the country paying his salary—by abusing a critical national security screening tool.

Five years later, in August 2006, several defendants of Tamil origin were arrested and charged with, among other things, attempting to bribe a U.S. State Department official to remove the Liberation Tigers of Tamil Eelam (Tamil Tigers) from the State Department's Foreign Terrorist Organization list.[52] The bribe offered was a reported US$1 million advance payment, a more lucrative package than Garcia had negotiated for himself. In a related case, jointly investigated by the U.S. Federal Bureau of Investigation (FBI) and the Royal Canadian Mounted Police, two residents of Montreal with ties to the Tamil terrorist organization were arrested after offering bribes to an undercover agent for assistance in smuggling non-Americans into the United States.[53]

In a more sophisticated scheme, Robert Schofield, an adjudications officer for the Department of Homeland Security's U.S. Citizenship and Immigration Services pleaded guilty on November 20, 2006, to selling United States immigration documents over an eight-year period. These documents, although illegally obtained, were authentic and enabled at least 184 aliens to receive naturalized U.S. citizenship.[54] Schofield was sentenced on April 20, 2007, to fifteen years in prison for bribery and ten years in prison for Naturalization Fraud; the sentences will run concurrently.[55]

While Garcia was selling access on the northern front, promiscuously corrupt Mexican officials were doing the same to the south: "For their part, unscrupulous officials exact bribes or *mordidas* from the Central Americans. The payments may be a few dollars to allow a single person to cross the border or thousands of dollars to permit the passage of drugs, weapons, stolen automobiles, prostitutes, exotic animals or archeological artifacts."[56] This problem straddles both sides of that border.

In the summer of 2006, two supervisory agents with the U.S. Border Patrol pleaded guilty for accepting bribes totaling almost US$200,000 in exchange for releasing smugglers and illegal immigrants from detention.[57] Another two agents were indicted for permitting illegal immigrants into the country in exchange for bribes.[58]

The United States requested nearly $8 billion in FY2007 for efforts to secure the nation's borders.[59] If access to the United States can be so easily and inexpensively purchased, why would a criminal or terrorist brave a direct attempt on the American system? If stories of bribe-taking officials can be found in the newspapers of any state with a land border, how can the country be kept secure? One former official at the U.S. Citizenship and Immigration Services expressed frustration, "[a]fter the next attack, when they find out that an employee was bribed by a terrorist or bribed by a spy, it's going to be too late," and resignation, "[i]n fact, I think it is too late."[60] Government officials who have grown fat on the bribes that facilitate narco-trafficking, human smuggling, and the illicit arms trade, seem unlikely to develop a conscience in the face of terrorists.

Hydro Kleen's tactics in Canada are distinguishable from the two Chechnyan women who bought their way past Russian airport security only in the ultimate goal and, presumably, the ultimate goal was not known to the airport officials that pocketed their modest bribe at the Moscow airport in the Chechynan case. The airport officials of many nations have a price and the price in these cases isn't very high.

Chapter 3

Gifts, Favors, and Hospitality

And thou shalt take no gift: for the gift blindeth the wise.

—Exodus 23: 8, King James version

GIFTS THAT KEEP ON GIVING

Gifts are important to the corrupt. They add a veneer of respectability to otherwise illicit transactions. Bribes are easy to condemn, but must gifts also be abolished? Is it really necessary to strip international business of all of its pleasure and camaraderie? It probably makes sense to begin by distinguishing gifts from bribes, to the extent that is possible. When the recipient of a gift or a favor is a government official with authority to make business decisions for the government, the distinction becomes especially important.

A gift, as opposed to a bribe, is generally thought to be a benefit that imposes no obligation on the recipient. A gift "is meant as an expression of personal affection, or some degree of love. It is given in a context created by personal relations to convey a personal feeling."[1] Some argue that the appropriate test is whether there is an explicit *quid pro quo*—an exchange—between the parties.[2] This definition is not a perfect fit for use in the field of international business. That there is no explicit *quid pro quo* may simply mean that the business proposition is not yet well-developed. Any *quid pro quo* at all, it would seem, would interfere with the appropriate objectivity of a government official. A company determined to influence an official inappropriately may not be able to imagine the explicit benefit deliverable by a newly appointed head of defense procurement, but may nevertheless want to be first in line when contract procurement begins. The bribe-based relationship is being developed and primed in anticipation of future deals.[3]

In 1976, the then president of Lockheed Martin, A. Carl Kotchian, testified before the Church Committee of the U.S. Senate about payments and accounting irregularities associated with sales in Europe.

Referring to a payment of US$1 million dollars to His Royal Highness, Bernhard, Prince of the Netherlands, consort of Queen Juliana, Senator Church asked Kotchian if he would characterize the payment as a bribe. Kotchian responded: "I think, sir, that as my understanding of a bribe is a quid pro quo for a specific item in return . . . I would characterize this more as a gift. But I don't want to quibble with you, sir."[4]

It is difficult to imagine that the representative of a multinational company would purchase any gifts other than the most modest and promotional unless he expected it to ingratiate him to the government official, his future customer, in some real and lasting way. Indeed, if there is truly nothing tangible to be derived from providing a gift or paying for dinner, it should follow that companies, which are not inherently philanthropic in structure and which are answerable to shareholders, should reconsider participating in gift-giving of any kind.

In the murky world of bribery, an initial willingness to offer gifts or to respond to requests for gifts may be the price of being dealt into the first round.[5] A lavish gift at the outset of a business relationship may be perceived by some as an indication that the giver is both in a position to and willing to garner corporate funds for additional, future "relationship-building" gestures. Executives of multinationals with policies prohibiting anything other than nominal gift-giving complain that initial meetings with new customers are more challenging if they do not arrive armed with goodies. Most agree that they are still able to do business with the customer, but that there is an initial hurdle to overcome.[6] On the other hand, executives of companies adopting a more restrictive policy after years of lavish gift-giving report soured relations when the gifts grow more modest or stop altogether. It presumably would be difficult, for example, to resume more modest gift-giving habits after providing a key customer with a solid gold model airplane[7]—surely the ultimate marketing item for an aerospace company— a Rolls-Royce,[8] fur coats,[9] or college tuition for their children,[10] but there is a vast grey area between company pens and a free ride through college. Reports from those working in the field indicate that with both expediting payments and gifts, companies new to a market should begin as they intend to continue, establishing a clear policy and adhering to it strictly.

In addition to the definitional challenges that arise when gifts and other benefits are discussed in a commercial context, there is the problem of determining whose judgment should prevail as to the reasonableness of the request, the value of the gift or favor delivered, and the intentions of the giver. If, as is often the case, a government official from a developing country asks for assistance in obtaining a visa for his daughter to work in the United States or assistance with her college applications, the cost of that favor may be zero to the company asked. The value to the official, however, may be very great indeed.

In one instance, a Lebanese official asked a representative of a U.S. multinational company for help in securing a visa appointment for a close friend.[11] At the time, the Consular Section of the U.S. Embassy in Beirut was closed and residents of Lebanon were required to travel to Damascus for their visas. Although the distance is just fifty miles, the drive is through the Bekaa Valley, with an unfriendly border crossing. In 1998, what awaited residents of Lebanon at the end of the drive was a long queue on the sun-baked sidewalk in front of the embassy. People often waited all morning only to have the line close in front of them and be instructed to return the next day. Under special circumstances, the embassy will schedule appointments which enable the applicant to avoid waiting in line.

If a company has good relations with an embassy, it may be able to secure such a visa appointment. It would cost the company nothing to be helpful to the government official in this way. For the official to secure the appointment for his friend in a timely manner would have been far more difficult, perhaps impossible. Should the price of the gift or favor be determined by its value to the giver or to the recipient? Timely access to U.S. consular services would certainly enhance an official's reputation. The official in the Lebanese case had extraordinary personal wealth and, arguably, would have been more impressed and influenced by this gesture than by a gift of several hundred dollars' value.

There is also a question of the relative value of a gift. A US$100 gift means very different things to an official in Bangladesh as compared to one in Japan, for whom it barely covers the cost of a single perfect, gift-wrapped melon. A self-proclaimed savvy businessman in Dubai attended an anti-bribery workshop there and cornered the speaker.[12] He stated that he had a close friend in the government of the United Arab Emirates who had a personal fortune of "billions" of dollars. As he explained, "I would humiliate myself if I gave him a gift worth less than a thousand dollars. This pen," (withdrawing a Mont Blanc pen of obvious value from his pocket), "this pen would be an embarrassment between us." Even if we set aside the possibility that the gentleman's friend had accumulated a portion of his wealth precisely because representatives of the business community were too *embarrassed* to give him gifts worth less than a thousand dollars, should companies consider the wealth of the recipient of hospitality or a gift? Are the means of a customer relevant to a question of abuse of authority? Are gifts of this value a good use of a company's resources?

Companies with international operations truly struggle with these issues. Some have been reduced to giving the tackiest gifts imaginable in the hope that they can keep up with their corporate peers and engage in a purported goodwill gesture that *won't* get them into trouble. Surely, they ask, if we give a foreign official a baseball cap with a big corporate logo on the front, no one will accuse us of bribery? The value of the

item, and whether it has any resale value, is probably useful information, but most anti-bribery laws have no minimum threshold, so even
the cheapest corporate giveaway can technically constitute a bribe if
the giver's intentions are to influence the official inappropriately. No
one is quite clear on the distinction between appropriate and inappropriate influence in this context. Setting aside whether the judgment of
any self-respecting government official can be purchased with a US$10
baseball cap when that sport—and fashion—are baffling to most non-
Americans, this is an area of constant and exhausting concern.

THE LUNAR NEW YEAR

Too often, what initially seems innocuous soon appears, at best,
ambiguous. At an anti-bribery conference in Shanghai, businessmen
operating in a region where gift-giving is a longstanding and entrenched
custom were looking for guidance and comfort.[13] First, they faced the
dilemma of *hong bao*, the decorative red envelopes into which cash is
placed and which are then given to family members, colleagues, and
customers to celebrate the Lunar New Year. Accounts of *hong bao* date
back more than a thousand years to the Sung Dynasty in China. This
question is always raised in countries with large Chinese populations
and the lawyers' response is always the same: regardless of the venerable nature of this custom, do you want to have to explain to a jury of
your peers the good intentions, purity of heart, and cultural sensitiv-
ity that motivated you to slip cash into an opaque envelope and hand
it over to a government official in a position to award you business?
Probably not. Instead, if gift-giving is appropriate, wouldn't it be pru-
dent to give something with no resale value? The ideal gift, it seems,
would be a modest, perishable product that expressed the goodwill of
the company, but couldn't be construed as a bribe—something like a
moon cake.
    Moon cakes are a bit like an elaborately filled cookie. They can be
filled with almost anything: nuts, seeds, ham, or preserved eggs. They
are exchanged, as the name suggests, during the Moon Festival. But the
moon cake industry has run amok. A report on the trend states that
"the tradition, more than 1,000 years old, has been much eclipsed in
recent years as over-packaging has made the moon cake and its symbolic meaning merely a side dish to an extravagant trend."[14] In this
article, manufacturers of "luxury moon cakes" were interviewed and
they indicated, not surprisingly, that most of their customers are large
companies hoping to impress customers: "Some of the more exotic and
pricey moon cakes include those filled with shark fin or packaged with
gold bars."[15] *Gold bars!* These gift boxes cost about US$1,210. So much
for cookies, but at least they are perishable and so—without the gold

bars—carry little resale value. And, after all, how many moon cakes can one government official eat?

It seems that, around the time of the Moon Festival, some government officials send their staff down to the terrace in front of their ministry offices where, with hammers and plywood, they erect small, makeshift stalls.[16] The employees are then expected to man these stalls, where they'll spend the next week or so hawking the very moon cakes that their venerable employers have received—or extorted—as gifts. It may be the case that no one in China actually eats moon cakes anymore and that, for a brief period each year, they form a strange, second currency.

For corporations, moon cakes had been treated like the Asian equivalent of a baseball cap bearing a corporate logo or a faux leather folio. Instead, these modest and endearing holiday cookies turn out to be gold-plated, in some cases quite literally.

More disturbing than a scheme that turns a beloved thousand-year tradition into a squalid wholesale operation, more disturbing even than officials using their office and staff first to solicit these gifts and later to resell them, was the way this scheme came to the attention of the public. Several years ago, it was rumored that some government officials reluctant to forego the additional revenue kept moon cakes that were unsold at the end of the last Lunar New Year and attempted to sell them the following year, resulting in several cases of severe food poisoning.

NIGERIAN GOATS

A year after the anti-bribery conference in China, where the moon cake resale scheme was discussed, there was a similar conference held in Lagos. Nigeria is often—and occasionally unfairly—the butt of bribery jokes; this is not only because of the Abacha legacy, but also because of that country's association with phony fax and e-mail schemes promising to give the participant a cut if they'll help some wealthy former official launder the millions he was able to filch while in office.

Given the desire of expats to discuss the challenging working conditions in their adopted home and the desire of the locals to exonerate themselves, the Lagos conference was expected to be lively, but the speakers were taken by surprise when the discussions focused primarily on goats.

The end of the Moslem period of pilgrimage to Mecca each year is marked by Eid ul-Adha. During this Islamic festival, wealthy Moslems sacrifice a sheep or goat as a symbol of Ibrahim's sacrifice. The meat of the animal sacrificed is shared with family, neighbors, and the less fortunate, in accordance with Islamic principles of charity.

The Niger Delta, in the southwestern corner of Nigeria, is characterized by warring traditional leaders, roving gangs, the absence of any
discernible rule of law and, relevant for our purposes, the sabotage of
oil and gas facilities and kidnapping of employees of multinational
companies operating there.[17] The Delta is also home to a significant
Moslem population. Because the extractive industry must follow the
resources, many major oil companies and the hundreds of companies
that support them are active in the Niger Delta.

As Eid ul-Adha approaches, traditional leaders begin to make their
expectations known. They require between twenty and forty goats, as
a gesture of goodwill and in accordance with their stature in the community. It's difficult to assess the street value of a Nigerian goat, but
goats clearly have symbolic value for the traditional leaders in this part
of the world and are distributed in an elaborate form of patronage.

The goats, like the moon cakes, become a form of currency. Tribal
leaders can sell them or bestow them on faithful followers in order
to consolidate or extend their authority. Whereas the gilded moon
cakes bring with them an expectation of new business, the goats buy a
respite from threatened sabotage and worse. Is there a one-to-one cor-
relation? Does each moon cake produce a new contract and each goat
a week without incident? Of course not. But each tainted transaction
of this kind erodes the reputation of the country involved—and China
and Nigeria are already among the worst—undermines the confidence
of foreign investors, and exacerbates the sheer hassle for companies
considering business opportunities. One senior executive once con-
fided in me that his company would do business in Nigeria "over [his]
dead body." Nigeria is a country rich in resources, but major multinational companies walk away because of the goat factor and all that it
represents.

THE AMBIGUOUS BECOMES OUTRAGEOUS: AZERBAIJAN

But while it is possible that gift-giving can benefit generous companies, it is plain that gift-giving can also backfire, even for the very
sophisticated businessman. This is certainly true for Viktor Kozeny, a
Czech citizen dubbed the Pirate of Prague by Fortune Magazine.[18] In
October 2005, the wildly successful Kozeny was indicted in the southern district of New York for, among other things, conspiracy to violate
the FCPA.[19] Kozeny is accused of having bribed officials of the Republic of Azerbaijan to gain advantages associated with a privatization
voucher program. Kozeny is alleged to have provided Azeri officials
with designer clothing, medical expenses, and travel by private jet, in
addition to millions of dollars in cash and wire transfers. But one allegation stands out from the rest for ostentation: in May 1998, Kozeny is

accused of arranging to have a representative of the British jeweler to members of the Royal Family, Asprey & Garrard, fly to Azerbaijan with six lavish gifts worth more than US$600,000, including an enamel box encrusted with diamonds worth about US$383,000 and an 18k photo frame with clock worth about US$44,000. Upon arrival, Kozeny is said to have selected one item, a black, monogrammed alligator desk set, as his gift to a senior Azeri official on the occasion of his birthday. The remaining five pieces were then allegedly passed amongst the other officials who were urged to select gifts to offer their feted official on their own behalf, apparently rendering each a "double bribe."[20]

FUR COAT IN LONDON

Entrepreneurial bribe-takers may involve their spouses to strengthen their negotiating position. Indeed, the sense of entitlement of spouses occasionally rivals that of the government official. Imelda Marcos, former first lady of the Philippines, is still thought to have been the mastermind behind her husband's looting spree, and less lofty spouses are routinely invoked by officials willing to ask for goodies on their behalf.

A London-based company was in the final stages of negotiating a major contract with a mid-level Polish government official.[21] The English businessman had offered repeatedly to travel to Poland for discussions, but the Polish official had always declined, stating that he was happy for the excuse to travel to London for meetings. His wife always traveled with him; she shopped while he worked. They added a day or two to their trips for relaxation.

As the details of the deal were slowly transformed into contract language, the Polish official grew increasingly vague and appeared to lose his commitment to the transaction. He indicated that there were still a number of items that needed further deliberation. He refused to continue discussions and asked that all remaining issues be deferred until a future trip. He added that he didn't want to return without his wife, but that his wife found London uncomfortably cold. Alas, he asked ruefully, how could this be resolved?

Setting aside the alarm bells that should have gone off when a Polish woman complained about English winters, the English businessman had a few options at this point. He might have repeated his offer to travel to Poland for the next meeting. He might have suggested that they meet in a third, presumably temperate, location. Instead, he asked solicitously what could be done to make the customer's wife more comfortable and learned that her discomfort could be easily remedied with a full-length fur coat. With a fur coat, he was assured, she would be very comfortable and negotiations could be resumed and concluded.

Notwithstanding those "savvy" operators who dole out facilitating payments to everyone they encounter upon stepping off the plane and contrary to media accounts, it is rare for businessmen to seek out government officials to bribe. Bribery is risky. In some countries, the offense of bribery carries the death penalty. Bribe-payers face the possibility of execution in only a handful of countries, but in many more prison time is a real risk. Bribery is bad for business; it buys an unenforceable contract. If a company provides lavish gifts in order to win a contract and the official reneges on the deal or is removed from office before he can follow through, there is no legal recourse. Few courts will be sympathetic to the argument that the company deserves the benefit of its illegal deal and that criminals should be compelled to see their crimes through to completion. Bribery is bad for public relations. When a government official agrees to buy inferior products at inflated prices because there's a benefit in it for him, he violates all obligations to the citizens he purportedly represents and they won't thank him—or the complicit company that made it all possible.

A businessman representing a successful, reputable company will generally prefer markets in which the best products sell at the best price without the risk, expense, and hassle of bribery.[22] If this is true in most cases—and it certainly doesn't address the criminally-minded, or businessmen selling hopelessly inferior or expensive products or employees desperate to make their marketing goals at any cost—why do so many companies play along?

The Polish official waited until the deal was almost concluded. A camaraderie had developed, presumably, and a shared investment in the outcome. Sunk costs had accumulated, and personal relationships had been established. It grows increasingly difficult to walk away from a deal as the time spent nurturing it increases.

THE PROBLEM WITH COMMITTEES

It is often the case that businessmen do not fully understand the nature of the business environment in which they are operating until negotiations are quite far along. A western businessman active in one of the poorest of the Middle Eastern countries describes the problem of committees.[23] The officials of this country love committees and the prestige of grand titles. Three of these officials—all fairly junior, but key decision-makers for the company's contracts—approached the company with a proposal to help demonstrate its commitment to the community by establishing and funding a new nonprofit committee to explore economic development. New to the country, the country manager had some discretionary funds for community relations. Unable to find any flaw in the proposal and eager to please an important government customer, he agreed.

The three gentlemen returned several weeks later. They had given the committee a great deal of thought, they said, and were excited about its potential. They had also decided who should serve on the committee. They handed over a list, turned and left.

The three government officials had listed themselves for the committee, together with three of their relatives and the country manager. The country manager took comfort from the fact that the committee was to be established as a nonprofit entity and that the underlying purpose of poverty alleviation remained worthwhile.

Two or three weeks later, the gentlemen paid another visit to the office. They had discussed logistics amongst themselves, it unfolded, and had concluded that Paris was the best location for meetings of the committee. They were in agreement that holding meetings in Paris would ensure they had everyone's undivided attention. Taken aback, the country manager asked a few questions about how many days should be set aside and whether his company's contribution would be needed to cover travel cost. It was generally agreed that five days would be sufficient and that the lofty members of the committee could not be expected to pay their own expenses.

Several more weeks passed until the country manager looked up again, wearily, to see his principal customers and fellow committee members standing in his reception area. He ushered them into his office. They had been talking amongst themselves and were very excited about this grand new committee which had, to date, accomplished nothing at all. They had concluded, however, that it would be appropriate, in light of the senior people they had been able to attract, to pay an honorarium commensurate with their rank.

The whole gentle scheme, it seemed, had been borne out of a shared goal to spin their modest standing in the government into all-expenses-paid trips to Paris with spending money. The problems for the company were two-fold. First, they had permitted things to develop in a manner that was difficult to reverse and, with no intention of bribing anyone, they found themselves in the dubious legal position of flying key customers to European capitals flush with an unearned honorarium. Of equally pressing concern, there were competitors waiting on the sidelines to step in and fill any vacuum left by the customers' sudden change of heart should they be disappointed.

In other cases, companies have been asked or encouraged to contribute to "social programs" of questionable structure and purpose,[24] to the charities of a government official's choice[25] and, in the aftermath of earthquakes and other natural disasters, to questionable disaster relief projects.[26] As a sovereign state, a government customer is free to demand whatever legal benefits they choose in contract negotiations. Oil and gas companies, for example, are routinely required to undertake infrastructure projects as a part of production sharing contracts and defense companies are accustomed to demands for "offsets"—commitments to undertake local investment or to purchase local content as a part of the contract.[27] There is a distinction, however, between agreeing to build a hospital or hire 500 local employees in principal and agreeing to do either in the jurisdiction where a key customer is up for reelection.

ALL IN THE FAMILY

Many mid-level government officials seem to have a secret manual for low-grade bribery schemes of this kind, taking advantage of company employees who are already keen to please and are grasping at any legitimate way to generate goodwill. What company executive would balk at the opportunity to advise a government official's daughter on the most appropriate choice of colleges back in the United States? But before long, the offer of help has been stretched to include the office staff editing her admissions essay and letters of recommendation until, finally, the official asks if the company has a scholarship program and mightn't his daughter be eligible?

In two very similar situations originating in different countries, government officials approached companies that had a great deal to lose from the officials' displeasure.[28] In each situation, the request started with a description of an ailing relative in need of medical assistance in the West. Early discussions were about the best hospitals and the best doctors until, slowly, it was made clear that the relative was in need of urgent care and the official couldn't afford it. The rest was left hanging, unspoken, in the air between them. In the second scenario it was suggested that the businessman, with his network of international contacts, might be well-positioned to help *procure* a kidney for an urgently needed transplant. Setting aside the disturbing issues that arise out of trafficking in human organs, the company in this case was appealed to on grounds of humanitarian need and corporate citizenship in spite of the underlying illegality of the proposal. The representative of the company that recounted this demand believed that willingness to grant this "favor" would determine the big winner in a pending government contract.

The gifts and favors that officials hint at for themselves and their family members are without limit. They run the course from the mundane to the very imaginative, but they are rarely spontaneous. As in the case of our committee-loving friends in the Middle East, the process is often carefully orchestrated to raise the stakes slowly over time.

BIDDING FAVORS

When a Minister of Defense is bribed to buy dilapidated Russian jets with no readily available spare parts instead of new and better French jets and further agrees to pay twice as much for them, the wrongdoing is clear. The Minister, in this case, has spent more of his country's resources to buy an inferior product in order to enrich himself, and each citizen of that country is a little worse off as a result. If the country faces a war, of course, the citizens may be considerably worse off as a result of his treachery.

One U.S. company describes competition for a contract to install a state-of-the-art air traffic control system in a Latin American country.[29] The quality of the air traffic control system and its coverage can determine future revenues for the host country as its government collects the overflight fees paid by carriers crossing its air space. As such, while the initial expense is great, the investment can become profitable over time, while also increasing air safety and improving a nation's image worldwide for its commitment to secure international travel.

In this case, the host country used a two-part bid process. Bids were first graded on the basis of technical quality and only after were prices, kept secret until completion of the first round, considered. This is thought to be a fairer, more transparent system because it requires any bribe-payer to influence both committees. Throughout the tender and bid process, one company in particular was described as entertaining all government officials associated with the project almost constantly and in great style.

The company selected, the company that entertained in such lavish style, turned out to be the company with the lowest technical grade and the highest price. Apparently, even the two-part bid system was not sufficient to throw off corrupt market forces in this case. The competitors complained and the whole project was cancelled, leaving the companies with no return on their considerable investment in the bid process, leaving the citizens of the country with an antiquated air traffic control system and leaving international travelers less secure. It is suggested by some that the hospitality provided was just one symptom of much greater bribery and that large traditional bribes almost certainly changed hands. This may be true, but if it is it would seem to support the position that a company that starts down the path of gifts and favors—and the government officials who encourage it—is, either deliberately or naively, initiating a commercial arrangement from which it is difficult to pull back.

A SLIPPERY SLOPE

It isn't clear whether gift-giving, when it gets out of hand, is a problem that lies more with the giver or the recipient. Businessmen generally concede that they are comfortable with gift-giving and hospitality when the expectations are clear and not patently inappropriate and when they're able to feel pleasantly generous rather than socially awkward. When pressed, however, the anecdotes flow freely.

One businessman described a meticulously orchestrated dinner to which a government official had been invited for what was billed as a fairly ordinary relationship-building meal. A budget had been established for the dinner and the restaurant carefully chosen. When the official arrived, however, he was accompanied by what could only be described as an entourage. The official spoke to the waiter in the local language, which his host did not speak. A special wine list appeared and the guest proceeded to order bottles of wine worth more than the average monthly wages of his countrymen. The businessman had tried to manage the situation, but was left with a bill for many thousands of dollars. It is difficult to imagine what alternatives were open to him once his guest and possible future customer set his sights on a lavish evening. At the same time, it is easy to imagine that this businessman might expect more such evenings in his future once the tone was set. This sort of erosion of corporate governance, willing or otherwise, is a hallmark of providing benefits to government officials and the slope grows very slippery indeed.

Government officials from certain developing countries are notorious for embarking on legitimate business trips penniless and then turning to their hosts upon arrival with expectant looks and upturned hands. A host company can't leave them at their hotels to amuse themselves between meetings with no cash for meals, much less taxi fare or spending money. It's a real and widespread dilemma that each company must address, but even this can be taken to absurd extremes. In one case, an official apparently had funds to rent a fast car and run up a startling bar bill and the combination landed him in jail with bail set high in recognition of his "flight risk."[30] The official called the company that had invited him and explained that they would have to post bail, surely "something of value" in the mind of the imprisoned official. Hoping to avoid an embarrassing international incident that centered on a key customer, the company paid. The official promptly jumped bail and hopped a plane home.

Perhaps more worrying still was a situation described by a company on the United States' west coast that hosted an official who spent every spare moment shopping maniacally. At the end of his week of meetings, he delivered several large, sealed trunks to the offices with a note instructing the company to ship them home for him as there was too much to take with him on his flight. The company was faced with the unpleasant prospect of over a thousand dollars in shipping costs for items it would either have to label falsely, not knowing what was inside, or unpack and identify.

When you add sweetheart deals, prostitutes, and pedicures to goats, and human body parts—it is a parade of horrors for a corporate compliance officer and even worse for a public relations office if the news breaks. Baseball caps bearing the company's logo are unlikely ever to land a company in trouble, but the vast uncharted land between the extremes can send a confusing message to government officials, and confusion is a state in which most shady officials prosper.

Chapter 4

Undermining Confidence in Government

In the end, if the people cannot trust their government to do the job for which it exists —to protect them and to promote their common welfare —all else is lost.

—Senator Barack Obama, speech at the Nairobi University, August 28, 2006

BITING THE HAND THAT FEEDS

So far this book has focused on wrongdoing by government officials. Their thefts, subversions and distortions of good business practices and good governance are harmful enough in themselves, but this chapter will argue that these criminal acts, taken together, have a much more significant and more destructive impact. Collectively, these misdeeds diminish the capacity of governments to deliver the basic goods of security and order.

In a primitive and shallow fashion, political power can be rooted in the simple fact that those in charge are able to summon up enough physical force to overmaster any challengers. The officials possess what political scientists call "a monopoly of violence." This is an unstable kind of government, always subject to challenge by any other possessor of force or by anyone ready to resort to violence. It is the kind of crude authority possessed by a clan leader in Mogadishu who can summon up, arm and reward a militia of his clansmen and some mercenaries. Such governments tend to rule briefly, to govern badly and to end violently.

Governments that will last longer and govern more constructively must be preferred and not just feared by their people. They must have constituents, not subjects, and to win their preference and allegiance, it is crucial that they be seen to be clean and committed to forwarding the common good of the country. This does not mean they need to be paragons; they merely need to be preferable to the anarchic, exploitative, usually incompetent dictators that in many cases came before and might well return if the government falls.

The kind of corrupt behavior described in this book works power-fully to undermine the trust that can lead to allegiance and endow a regime with legitimacy. The more government officials use the power of the state to enrich themselves, the more they deplete the trust and confidence of the people under their control and the less durable and effective the power of the government will likely prove to be.

Unchecked corruption will almost inevitably render governments unable to deliver on even basic state functions of providing security, creating and maintaining education, transportation, communication, healthcare and sanitation systems, and enforcing the rule of law. Cor-ruption is most insidious in overturning the last and most crucial of these—the rule of law. In the end, a state run by bribe-takers will likely be reduced to a hollowed out kleptocracy, a husk of a state with no legitimacy or effectiveness. Such husks tend to collapse into state fail-ure or anarchy.

SIPHONING OFF RESOURCES AND DELIVERING INSECURITY

A government must provide some degree of physical security for its citizens by maintaining police and military forces. These can be beneficial institutions or predatory ones, protectors or parasites, and in a fundamental way it is their degree of corruption that influences the difference. The Roman emperor Caligula was said to have asked of his praetorian guard, "But who will guard the guards themselves?" (It was a good question; he was ultimately assassinated by his own guard.) The citizens of corrupt states must ask the same question. If their protec-tors are bribe-takers, they will prove more parasitic than protective.

Selling Out the Military

When the military is thoroughly corrupt, the path to utter state col-lapse and appalling violence is short. Consider the bloody civil war that gripped Sierra Leone in the 1990s with its horrifying atrocities, shady diamond deals, and recruitment of child soldiers on a massive scale. Many members of the government-sponsored armed forces of Sierra Leone found that illicit diamond mining was so profitable compared to their unreliable official salaries that they were happy to avoid combat and instead join the rebel forces in scouring the country-side for these mineral riches, or failing that, to loot civilian villages. Some units of this parasitic military ultimately attacked the national capital, Freetown, in 1997 in the chillingly and aptly named "Opera-tion No Living Thing."[1] Nigeria, Haiti, and the Philippines have, like

Liberia, descended into sheer kleptocracy, and the Democratic Republic of the Congo has approached utter collapse into violence and pillage.

It would be complacent and wrong to suppose that corruption hollows out only the institutions of underdeveloped states. At the opposite end of the spectrum from the military of Sierra Leone stands so respected an institution as the armed forces of the United States. The U.S. military prides itself on its high degree of professionalism, yet it too has experience with bribery. In the early days of the U.S. occupation of Iraq, billions of dollars earmarked for reconstruction projects flowed from the U.S. treasury to the Coalition Provisional Authority in Baghdad without adequate supervision. The opportunities inherent in this cash-rich, oversight-poor situation proved too tempting for some. In 2006, Bruce Hopfengardner, a lieutenant colonel in the U.S. Army Reserve, pleaded guilty to conspiracy charges related to his role in a scheme to steer lucrative reconstruction contracts to a Philip Bloom, an American businessman who was also convicted in the case, in exchange for a new car, a motorcycle, camera equipment, a computer, and an expensive watch.[2] According to the Special Inspector General for Iraq Reconstruction, the scheme involved not only outright theft, but also a conspiracy to make payments to Bloom's firm despite "defective or non-performance of contract terms."[3]

In this case, the U.S. government may have been trying to undertake a mammoth reconstruction effort in Iraq, but in at least one region where this conspiracy unfolded, the self-interest of U.S. officials trumped the mission, rendering U.S. efforts less effective and U.S. credibility tarnished. Corrupt practices chipped away at the prospects for success in an undertaking that has cost thousands of American lives and hundreds of billions of American dollars, and left the United States and its military significantly discredited in the eyes of the Iraqi people.

Sometimes the very officials responsible for ensuring that the taxpayers get the best quality at the best price abandon their duties in order to enrich themselves—even when their duties are intimately related to national security. In 2002, Darleen Druyun, a former principal deputy assistant secretary of defense and the number two acquisitions officer for the U.S. Air Force, was making plans for her next career. Boeing had proven congenial to date, hiring both her daughter and her future son-in-law. According to Druyun, she spoke frequently with representatives at Boeing, including discussions about her daughter's performance in her position at the company; she even received reports on her daughter's pay increases.[4] While communicating with Boeing about her daughter's employment and negotiating a vice president slot and US$250,000 annual salary for herself, Druyun was also negotiating a US$20 billion contract with Boeing on behalf of the U.S. government.[5] In awarding the contract, Druyun conceded that she "agreed to a higher price for the aircraft than she believed was appropriate" and that she did so as a "parting gift to Boeing."[6] As a final insult—this time directed at the private sector—she also admitted to passing to Boeing what she considered to be proprietary pricing data supplied by another aircraft manufacturer.[7] Druyun admits that she suffered a "loss of her objectivity" and "took actions which harmed the United States."[8] She also helped undercut the confidence and trust of the public in their government and in her subsequent corporate employer.

Indignant, the U.S. attorney for the Eastern District of Virginia sent a strong message on the case: "Darleen Druyun placed her personal interest over the interests of the Air Force and American taxpayers . . . Secretly negotiating employment with a government contractor, at the same time you are overseeing the negotiations of a multibillion dollar lease from the same contractor, strikes at the heart of the integrity of the acquisition process."[9] Druyun was sentenced to nine months imprisonment, seven months of community confinement, 150 hours of community service and a US$5,000 fine. Boeing's former chief financial officer, Michael Sears, also pleaded guilty for his role in the scandal.[10]

The Druyun case and the case involving Hopfengardner and Bloom were investigated and the rule of law, eventually, prevailed. But when countries less committed to transparency or endowed with less well established institutions are involved, outcomes are far less clear. For almost twenty years since the Soviet Union collapsed, the United States has been neck-and-neck with Russia in the competition to export defense items.[11] China and India are consistently the world's largest importers of these items, two countries with weak regulatory systems and low levels of transparency in procurement. These two countries inspire little confidence that weapons sold to them will not be resold to other, less friendly, states. Low levels of transparency in procurement, on the other hand, raise concerns about bribery-tainted major defense purchases. In light of rigorous export restrictions and in part because of remedial steps taken after the rash of bribery scandals in the 1970s and 1980s, most U.S. aerospace and defense multinationals are devoting considerable staff and resources to anti-bribery compliance.[12]

The defense industries of other countries, not having labored under comparably rigorous and expensive compliance requirements and as yet unchastened by prosecutors, often take a different approach. From mid-2004 through December 2006, British defense company BAE was under investigation by the United Kingdom's Serious Fraud Office (SFO) for possible bribes to members of the Saudi royal family in connection with the Al Yamamah ("the Dove") contract for, initially, Tornados and Hawk trainers and, later, Eurofighter Typhoons. Five people were taken into custody in the course of the investigation[13] and the list of allegations included a £60 million (US$118 million) slush fund from which payments were made to Saudi government officials, as well as gifts including a Rolls-Royce, all expense paid shopping trips at swanky shopping centers, and luxury travel.[14] The investigation picked up steam when it looked like the SFO would succeed in gaining access to bank accounts in Berne, Switzerland, and would finally be able to determine in whose hands the money ended up.

Investigations into behavior of this kind are slowly gaining momentum in Europe, but this one turned into an international incident. The Saudis reportedly threatened to terminate the contract in question and suspend diplomatic ties with Britain unless the SFO ended the investigation.[15] To show they were serious, they began discussions in early December 2006 with French company Dassault about the possibility of purchasing the Rafale, a competitor of BAE's Eurofighter.[16] The threats were hardly trivial; the BAE contract keeps 9,000 Britons employed. BAE estimates put earnings from the contract to date at £43 billion[17] (US$84 billion) and it is thought that the current contract could ultimately contribute another £40 billion (US$78 billion) to the British economy.[18]

In keeping with the complicated web of relationships that can be affected by bribes, Saudi Arabia, a country that has suffered directly from terrorist attacks and a key ally of the United Kingdom, also threatened to end intelligence cooperation with Britain in the effort to contain Al-Qaeda-led terrorism.[19] This is made more surprising by the fact that Al-Qaeda threatens Saudi interests, just as it does British interests. In this case, it appears that protecting the interest of the corrupt came into direct conflict with both commercial transparency and fundamental national security imperatives.

Bribery in the Mexican military takes a different shape. As a result of the propensity for some in the Mexican police force to protect and support narco-traffickers, the Mexican government expanded the role of the military in this area. Predictably, "[e]vidence suggests that drug corruption will move from one institution to the other, and that corruption will overwhelm the Mexican military long before the military curtails the drug trade."[20] When the military are paid badly and drug profits are enormous, the temptation to "cash in" on your enforcement authority can dominate other loyalties.[21] Even the country's first military officer to lead the war on drugs betrayed his country. General Jesús Gutiérrez Rebollo, famed to be tough and incorruptible,[22] was appointed commissioner of the Mexican National Institute to Combat Drugs in 1996. In 1997, less than a year after his appointment to the post, he was arrested, convicted, and sentenced to forty years in prison for providing protection to the leader of the most powerful Mexican drug cartel, cocaine kingpin Amado Carrillo Fuentes, known locally as the "Lord of the Skies." Informants stated that General Rebollo offered to send soldiers to protect the cartel's smuggling operations in return for US$60 million.[23] According to Mexico's then Defense Secretary, General Enrique Cervantes, General Rebollo "deceived his superiors, defrauded the confidence they placed in him, worked against Mexico's national security and damaged the combined institutional forces against narcotics trafficking."[24]

Public Health

States provide security from many threats through military and law enforcement mechanisms, but other dangers, such as infectious disease, require other governmental entities to hold them at bay. The avian influenza virus H5N1 has the international public health community worried.[25] It is thought by some to be "among the greatest threats to our country today."[26] Spread by domestic fowl and wild birds, the disease has occasionally mutated to infect humans, with a fatality rate in those cases of more than 50 percent. More than 100 people have died as a result of this emergent public health risk,[27] and there currently is no commercially available vaccine to protect against the virus.[28] While the medical research community scrambles to develop and test a vaccine, the World Health Organization and others work to contain the spread of the virus by, among other strategies, culling large numbers of birds in areas where the virus has been detected. Pandemics require cooperation within and between governments and, as with many critical government services, progress depends upon the integrity of the officials managing the process, from verification, through culling and coordinated medical care.

In Asia, the first line of defense against avian flu—the culling process— has repeatedly been undermined by farmers prepared to bribe cullers to spare their flocks.[29] One United Nations representative described the need for "an international culling task force" and, specifically, an "incorruptible public service to go around killing chickens."[30] Such a force would challenge national sovereignty and excite local resistance even before it began to thread its way through a thicket of bribe-offering opponents.

If the disease cannot be stopped at its source by the first line of defense, the larger public health system comes into play. One of the most likely vehicles for the spread of this pandemic flu virus is the commercial poultry trade[31] and regulation of the poultry trade gives rise to new fields of bribery. In early 2006, for example, the head of Moscow's Administration of Federal Service for Veterinary and Plant Oversight was arrested for trying to secure a US$25,000 bribe in exchange for permitting the sale in Moscow of 600 tons of Ukrainian chicken meat, banned because of avian flu fears arising out of recent cases in the Ukraine.[32] In cases such as this, corruption in one country's government can result in risks to the health and safety of citizens of many others.

The potential for corruption to worsen the effects of infectious disease is not hypothetical. To take a single case in point, Laurie Garrett has demonstrated that the systematic looting of Zaire—now the Democratic Republic of the Congo—that occurred during the Mobutu years dramatically exacerbated the human toll of the 1995 Ebola outbreak centered in the city of Kikwit. In her book *Betrayal of Trust: The Collapse of Global Public Health*, Garrett declared, "Two things are clear: Ebola spread in Kikwit because the most basic, essential elements of public health were nonexistent. And those exigencies were lacking in Kikwit—indeed, throughout Zaire—because Mobutu Sese Seko and his cronies had for three decades looted the national treasuries."[33] She also documents how, just a few years after the terrifying outbreak that killed 296 people, that corroding influence of corruption on public health systems was back with a vengeance. By 1998, a provincial governor had confiscated the region's only ambulance for his personal use.[34]

Even in less badly governed countries, the system for public health can be like a chain with every link for sale. First, in many countries public health officials must buy their positions. The World Bank surveyed public health officials in twenty-three developing countries and found that three-quarters of the government officials in Bosnia and Herzegovina who responded reported that a bribe is required simply to secure a job in the public health sector. Additional bribes are required for promotions. "In Ghana, 25 percent of health-sector jobs are 'for sale'."[35] At the peak of a dengue fever crisis in New Delhi in October 2002, the city lost the official "who completely oversaw the civic body's anti-malaria and anti-dengue campaigns."[36] The official was arrested for allegedly accepting a bribe of 2,000 Rupees (US$45) in exchange for securing a promotion for a subordinate. At a time when the city could least afford it, the scandal cost the community a key health worker and, presumably, undermined confidence in the integrity and governance within the municipal health office. "It is shameful that even during a crisis, [Municipal Corporation of Delhi] officials were trying to earn money on the sly."[37]

Once secure in their positions, public health officials have discretion to award contracts in the public interest, or to sell the good they are meant to provide. In 2003, Dr. Luo Yilu was presented with an award for curing more than 200 Severe Acute Respiratory Syndrome (SARS) patients during the epidemic in China that year.[38] He was considered one of several SARS heroes in China.[39] His hero status was shattered, however, when just three years later, he stood before the Haizhu District People's Court in Guangzhou and admitted to accepting thousands of yuan under the table from companies bidding on government contracts.[40] Similarly, Wang Xuewen, the director of the Pinggu Public Health Bureau was arrested for allegedly taking almost 100,000 yuan

(US$12,777) from a company selling sterilization equipment during the SARS outbreak.[41]

Luo Yaoxing, another key figure in the race to control SARS, was sentenced to life in prison in 2006 for accepting bribes totaling more than 11 million yuan (US$1.4 million) from vaccine producers at a time when he was authorized to approve all vaccine purchases in the province;[42] the Guangdong Province Disease Control Center Immunization Planning Institute that he once led petitioned the court for leniency in light of his record of public service. Luo returned the money, which he reportedly had stored in briefcases in an apartment he had rented for that purpose.[43]

An effective response to a public health emergency often depends upon the ability to move professionals and supplies to the affected area quickly. The facilitating payments described in Chapter 2 grow more serious when the need to negotiate with layers of bribe-takers prevents a timely response to a health emergency. One nongovernmental organization (NGO) reports that obstacles to transportation of medicine and emergency supplies, in particular, appear to be manufactured in proportion to the urgency in order to extort the largest possible payment from the NGO.[44]

Finally, public health officials, and especially state doctors, allocate resources. If government officials at each level skew contracts or skim benefits for themselves, it is difficult to imagine how anything is left for preventive measures or treatment of infectious disease, but there is one additional hurdle that citizens must clear. Doctors themselves often become more entrepreneur than healer; some start as early as medical school "where future doctors are graded according to the amount of money they give professors—and later treat people based on their ability to pay."[45]

The HIV/AIDS pandemic killed nearly 3 million people in 2006 alone. The disease is hollowing out whole communities, and prevention, care, and treatment efforts are still scrambling to catch up to the crisis. But this is especially difficult in countries where the entire public health infrastructure has been weakened by corruption. For example, in Ghana, only 20 percent of public nonwage funds budgeted for health clinics actually reach their destination.[46] In Shymkent, in southern Kazakhstan, many medical services are available only to those who pay bribes, including transfusions, medical procedures, and medicine. The region faces high levels of HIV/AIDS that require significant ongoing medical management as well as education with respect to transmission of the virus. But in the words of one observer, "Doctors converted all of this into a business: if you didn't pay a certain sum, it would mean they would treat you poorly, or they wouldn't see you at all. All of this fostered infection."[47] Effective government involvement within and across borders is critical if infectious diseases are to be tracked, slowed, and ultimately eradicated. Success in the field of public health can bolster public confidence just as failures of this kind can leave citizens bitter and cynical at best, and deathly ill at worst.

Protecting Natural Heritage

As is the case with critical public health initiatives, mismanagement and self-dealing by government officials can dramatically undermine the efficacy of programs designed to protect environmental resources. Sovereign states routinely make decisions about natural resources, controlling access and balancing the need for revenue with the desire, if any, for preservation. They also must decide how to balance the national interest in environmental regulation—air and water free of pollutants and toxins—with private sector interests that may perceive the regulation as overly intrusive or expensive. These are legitimate state decisions, although they may be governed in part by international conventions and may be subject to pressure from voters and from civil society. Inappropriate commercial pressures may also be brought to bear on individual decision-makers, tempting them to auction the authority of their government position for personal enrichment.

Monsanto, headquartered in Missouri, is a leading agricultural chemical company. In the Monsanto Pledge, rolled out in November 2000, the company committed to better business practices in, among other areas, environmental protection. Monsanto has a reputation as a good corporate citizen, but something went wrong in Indonesia.

Indonesia has a progressive environmental regulation requiring companies that seek to sell genetically-modified products in Indonesia to undertake and pay for an environmental impact study. Many countries have taken similar steps, insisting on regulation of these products.[48] Although there is significant disagreement on the risks associated with genetically modified products, it is squarely within a sovereign state's rights to regulate products with a potential impact on its agricultural sector.

In 2002, a manager at Monsanto appears to have concluded that the Indonesian environmental impact study was inappropriate, unnecessary, too onerous, or perhaps just inconvenient. He directed Monsanto's Indonesian consulting firm to pay US$50,000 to a senior official at the Indonesian Ministry of Environment to "incentivize" him to repeal the requirement.[49] He instructed the consultant not to discuss the matter with anyone else at Monsanto.[50] The consulting firm sent an employee to deliver the payment and the request for help. The Indonesian official promised to do what he could at the appropriate time. Here again, the scheme was accompanied by books and records violations and false invoices when the payment was characterized as "consultant fees."[51]

The official record makes it appear that the Indonesian official, again unnamed, kept the money, but ultimately declined to be of service to Monsanto. Presumably, it is more embarrassing to be a failed briber than a successful one, but the Indonesian official's role here is unique. He was the beneficiary of the widespread impression held by most businessmen that Indonesia suffers from rampant bribery and that important government decisions can be purchased. That impression landed this official US$50,000 in a country where the average annual income is about US$700. He did not, however, actually sell his public office for the intended end and did not, or perhaps could not, provide the Monsanto manager with the results he desired. Whether it is comforting to the people of Indonesia to have one of their government officials accept bribes but to renege on the illicit deal is unclear.

Back at Monsanto, the company entered into a nonprosecution agreement with the U.S. Department of Justice and a settlement agreement with the U.S. Securities and Exchange Commission (SEC), paid a fine of US$1.5 million, fired several employees in Indonesia, and agreed to hire an independent consultant to monitor its business practices worldwide for three years.[52]

Cambodia continues to struggle to recover from the environmental devastation wrought by Pol Pot's regime in the late 1970s. The government and NGOs active there are working to restore forests that were sold or stripped for food and firewood when the urban population was marched forcibly out of Cambodian cities and into the countryside. At the center of this important and heavily-funded reforestation project is Kham Khoeun, the former governor of Rattanakiri province and currently a fugitive from Cambodian law enforcement authorities.[53] Rattanakiri is a center for ecotourism and is home to Virachey National Park, created by Royal Decree in 1993. The park, about 200 miles northeast of the Cambodian capital, Phnom Penh, is managed by the Cambodian Ministry of the Environment and is part of the World Bank's biodiversity project. Kham Khoeun has been tried *in absentia*, convicted of accepting bribes in exchange for permitting illegal logging in Virachey National Park, and sentenced to prison.[54] Also sentenced were the province's former police chief, a park director, a provincial military chief, and several border guards. The bribery scheme was comprehensive, as were the damages assessed in compensation: US$15 million.[55]

Indonesia faces similar deforestation challenges. Western multinationals, sensitive to the campaigns of environmental nonprofit organizations, shy away from the reputational damage that operating in poorly regulated markets like Indonesia can bring.[56] Neighboring Malaysia has worked to develop a regulated logging industry that enables the Malaysians to sell timber to companies seeking to avoid the political and environmental issues surrounding Indonesian timber.

Taking advantage of this, Indonesian loggers need only bribe their way across the border to Borneo, where their wood can be labeled "Malaysian" and easily sold on the international market.[57] A single bribe-taker at the border, presumably in concert with others at each end of the transaction, can simultaneously thwart Indonesia's efforts to slow deforestation, reduce the revenue to Indonesia for its lumber—sold illicitly at reduced rates—and undermine Malaysian efforts to establish a credible timber industry through regulation.

Endangered species are put at additional risk by the practice of bribery. International trade in illegal wildlife products is estimated to be as high as US$10 billion annually.[58] Sariska National Park in the dusty western province of Rajasthan is one of twenty-eight small tiger reserves in India. After the numbers of tigers in India were seen to decline sharply until a 1972 census counted only 1,827 nationwide, then Prime Minister Indira Gandhi's government implemented protective measures in an effort to reverse the decline.[59] The tiger population began to recover until the 1980s, when demand grew for tiger bones used in traditional Chinese medicine and poachers began to move in to India. In 2005, the Indian government finally conceded that every tiger had disappeared from Sariska National Park.

Sansar Chand, described as a "notorious animal poacher," has been arrested for his part in wiping out the entire tiger population of Sariska reserve in under two years, completing the gruesome job sometime in late 2004 or early 2005.[60] India's Central Bureau of Investigation has recommended that staff be transferred out of the park, referring only to those who are "suspected to have developed vested interests."[61] Regardless of the level of cooperation that may or may not have occurred between national park rangers and the tiger poachers—and it is difficult to imagine losing every single tiger in the reserve to poachers without such collusion—the poachers almost certainly would have needed the cooperation of some government officials in India to transport the bones and the lucrative skins abroad.

The problem of pollution also appears in this parade of environmental horrors. On August 19, 2006, in the West African nation of the Ivory Coast, a large ship needed to unload hundreds of tons of chemical waste that contained hydrogen sulfide in concentrated doses.[62] A local company reportedly offered to dispose of the waste for less than US$20,000; the estimate from a European company had been sixteen times that. The local company's solution, apparently, was to dump the waste at seventeen sites around Abidjan, including residential neighborhoods.[63]

The government of the Ivory Coast launched an investigation and, according to one report, the commission has concluded that "corruption and negligence among a host of government officials, including Cabinet ministers and port workers, were to blame."[64] Elected and appointed government officials—public servants—facilitated the disposal of hundreds of tons of toxic waste killing ten people and sending another 100,000 to the hospital with unknown long-term consequences.

Also for sale in the world of bribe-seekers and bribe-payers are national treasures—the very manifestations of a people's history—found on the illicit international auction block. One startling example of how corruption can lead to the abdication of duty occurred in Egypt, where the three senior government archaeologists, appointed to protect the country's antiquities, were themselves arrested for accepting bribes in exchange for helping private buyers smuggle thousands of cultural treasures out of the country.[65] The scandal must have been a blow to national confidence in government, as well as to national pride.

Dipping into Public Resources

Governments collect revenues that are supposed to be devoted to the public good, and the most straightforward way for corruption to undermine the legitimacy of a governing regime involves public resources depleted directly by theft.

China struggles with this issue in part because of ineffective regulatory oversight of party and government leaders and in part because the government ignored the problem for so long that their indifference was thought tantamount to approval. The head of Shanghai's Communist Party, for example, has been fired based on allegations that he stole US$400 million of the city's pension fund.[66] Another senior government official in China recently received a life sentence for stealing US$3.2 million directly from the social security funds. He was also convicted of taking over US$100,000 in bribes. Once an official begins to abuse his office for personal gain, he rarely troubles himself with distinctions between direct theft and bribery. Interestingly, the official used the stolen money to play the stock market.[67]

In a similar spirit, the head of a township in southern China was sentenced to twenty years in jail after stealing US$13.9 million from the public till and then using the money to fund over 250 gambling trips to nearby Macau and Hong Kong, where he lost more than US$11 million of the money. He was also convicted of taking bribes in excess of US$200,000.[68]

The consequences of a food shortage that gripped parts of southern and eastern Africa in 2001 and 2002 were exacerbated in Malawi when the government sold its entire national grain reserve as the crisis began. The circumstances surrounding this decision were murky—and so was what happened to the proceeds from the sale. An independent Malawian newspaper "found the government sold the grain to dozens of companies, many of them newly registered firms owned by key figures in government"[69] and the county's own anti-corruption bureau recommended prosecuting officials who had mismanaged the grain reserves.[70] None of this was much help to the Malawian people who suffered and, in far too many cases, died during the famine.

UNDERMINING DEMOCRACY

Democratic governments derive their legitimacy not just from some abstract measure of their capacity to deliver services, but specifically from the will of the people. Officials are held accountable for their job performance in regular, credible elections, and if a given officeholder is not successful at the ballot box, he no longer has any claim to his post. But in some cases, corruption takes direct aim at democratic processes and institutions themselves, substituting the will of the bribe-paying for the will of the public at large.

Skewing Elections in Benin

In September 2003, Titan Corporation executives watched as their share price shot up 26 percent[71] and Lockheed Martin's lawyers swarmed over their San Diego corporate campus preparing to close on an acquisition that promised to be lucrative for all. A U.S. aerospace giant, Lockheed's history of paying bribes to secure lucrative contracts meant it was one of a handful of companies credited with giving the United States the FCPA.[72] The company also bumped up against the law after its enactment in 1977. Lockheed pled guilty in 1994 to conspiracy to violate the FCPA after it was uncovered that a sale to the Egyptian military of three C-130 Hercules planes was tainted by bribes totaling US$1 million.[73] Lockheed paid the largest fine in the history of the FCPA to settle the matter and that fine—a total criminal and civil settlement of US$24.8 million—held the record until 2005.

In the wake of the Egyptian incident, Lockheed put in place a rigorous anti-bribery compliance program and it brought this to bear on the proposed Titan acquisition. During the course of the acquisition investigation, anomalous payments were uncovered by the due diligence team in, among other countries, the Republic of Benin. Benin is a former French colony slightly smaller than Pennsylvania that lies directly west of Nigeria and southeast of Burkina Faso. Almost half of the population of eight million is under the age of fifteen and the country is dependent upon subsistence agriculture. Since gaining independence from France in 1960, Benin has toyed with military rule and socialism, but free elections were held in 1991 and the country has muddled through with a largely functional electoral system since then.

In 1996, Lieutenant Colonel Mathieu Kérékou defeated his predecessor and was elected president of Benin; he easily won re-election
in March 2001, where he remained until term limits prevented his re-
election in 2006. The March 2001 election was mired in controversy.
Kérékou won less than a majority of the votes in the first round. General
Christophe Soglo, who took second place, and Adrien Houngbedji, who
took third place, withdrew from the second round, alleging election
fraud. Kérékou was left to face only the fourth place contender in the
second round and won with 83.6 percent of the vote.

At the time of the 2001 election, Benin was an important market for
Titan, which was involved in modernizing the country's telecommuni-
cation infrastructure. Benin became even more important after Kérékou's victory, when the fees that Titan received for managing the project
were increased from 5 to 20 percent. This increase was documented in
an agreement signed on June 25, 2001, and made effective retroactive
to August 3, 1998.[74]

According to court documents, in 2001, at the direction of at least
one senior Titan officer, Titan poured more than US$2 million into
Benin to be used for President Kérékou's election campaign. This money
was in addition to millions more paid by Titan from 1999 to 2001 to
the company's local agent who was also, as luck would have it, the
President's "business advisor."[75] Approximately US$1 million worth
of payments nominally earmarked for "social programs" in Benin were
wired to the business advisor's offshore account in a notorious personal tax haven, the Principality of Monaco. Another US$1.1 million
was delivered to the business advisor in Benin in cash. As so often
happens in commercial bribery, the wrongdoing was exacerbated by
the usual allegations of inaccurate entries in the company's books and
records, falsified invoices, and shoddy internal controls more generally.[76] The court concluded that "virtually all" of the payments made
in 2001 were "funnelled to the re-election efforts of the Benin president." Some of the money was used to pay for re-election t-shirts
adorned with a picture of Kérékou and instructions to vote for him in
the upcoming election.

The corporate story ends with Lockheed Martin walking away from
its proposed US$2.4 billion acquisition of Titan.[77] Titan, having begun
the acquisition process celebrating a rapid increase in share price, found
itself just nine months later with no buyer, a reduced international
presence, a plummeting share price, and onerous remedial measures.
At US$28.5 million, Titan's fine finally replaced Lockheed's own as the
largest to date under the FCPA and held the record for two years until it
was trumped by Baker Hughes' US$44 million fine in April 2007.

The illegal business advantage purchased was short-lived. The decision of a handful of executives to win business by circumventing the
law wreaked havoc with the value and reputation of the company and

with its long-term prospects. Because of media attention, growing public intolerance, and prosecutorial zeal, Titan became a proxy for American companies more generally. Many companies that hadn't taken the issue seriously began to look at their own business practices and decide it was time to bolster internal compliance controls.[78]

Publicly available documents describe political contributions made by a major U.S. multinational in support of a sitting president, together with allegations that the company received a clear and immediate four-fold increase in compensation as a result. It seems clear that there were two sides to the wrongdoing. But in the strange, lopsided world of corporate anti-bribery enforcement, Titan pleaded guilty in March 2005 to three felony counts of violating the FCPA, but neither the Beninese agent, nor the president himself, is so much as named in the court documents and neither, to date, appears to have suffered any sanction for the scandal. The complaint submitted by the SEC in March 2005 refers to "Benin's then-incumbent president." At the time of filing, "then-incumbent" President Kérékou was still very much in power. There is no proof that the president's business advisor ever informed the president of the source of the multi-million dollar windfall, neither does it appear that anyone asked. The president presumably would have been aware of the company's munificence when it presented his wife with a pair of earrings valued at US$1,850. The Beninese government simply refused to comment.[79] In any case, the president and alleged beneficiary was able to retire at the end of his term-limited career without investigation or consequence. Yet the facts of the case lead one to wonder: just who was the president beholden to in his final term in office—the voters or the foreign company that bankrolled his campaign?

And in the Cook Islands

By comparison, the Cook Islands, a tiny parliamentary democracy, has shown little patience with bribery. Named for Captain Cook, the man who first sighted them in 1770 roughly halfway between Hawaii and New Zealand, the Cook Islands chose self-governance in 1965. This archipelago of fifteen islands, some mere coral atolls and some volcanic, was under the administrative control of New Zealand from 1900 through 1965 and there remain close ties and regular migration between the two countries. Indeed, emigration from the Cook Islands to New Zealand has been a cause of some concern, as the Islands have a negative population growth rate. The Cook Islands are formally a self-governing parliamentary democracy and elections are held every five years to select the prime minister. The country and its then-prime minister, Sir Albert Henry, faced such an election in 1978. With a population at that time of only 18,000, strong voter turnout was expected to affect the outcome and fairly small changes in the electorate could reverse the outcome.

At this time, Kenny International Corp. was a New York corporation run by its president and CEO, Finbar B. Kenny. Kenny International held an exclusive distribution agreement for the postage stamps of the Cook Islands, whereby the government of the islands received half of all revenue from the sales. Apparently a favorite of stamp collectors, the Cook Island philatelic contract generated annual revenue of about US$1.5 million. When Sir Albert scheduled the election, Kenny presumably concluded that his continuing stamp deal depended on the Prime Minister's victory. At a meeting scheduled between Kenny and a personal representative of the Prime Minister in Honolulu early in 1978, it was determined that Kenny could help secure a victory for Sir Albert by paying to bring Sir Albert's supporters back to the Cook Islands in order to vote in the election.[80] Kenny ultimately did provide transportation for voters, in violation of local and U.S. law, and it would appear that Sir Albert won the election as a direct result of the votes cast by those Kenny flew in. When the High Court of the Cook Islands uncovered the scheme and disallowed the "unlawful votes tainted by bribery,"[81] Sir Albert's party lost its control of the Legislative Assembly and Sir Albert was removed from office. Back in the United States, Kenny pleaded guilty to one count of bribery and paid a US$50,000 fine in one of the earliest FCPA enforcement actions.

CHECKING CORRUPTION: A SORDID INCIDENT VERSUS A DOWNWARD SLIDE

While government officials of all countries are susceptible to bribery, the examples in this chapter indicate that, in most cases, countries with high levels of transparency can weather these scandals more easily than those with a tradition of government secrecy. A robust democracy depends upon the public's access to information. Knowledgeable voters can keep an eye on the till, making informed decisions about public spending and holding their government officials accountable for their actions. In these states, when corruption is uncovered, the official responsible is typically fired and occasionally imprisoned and the news is made available to the public. In states without that degree of transparency and accountability, citizens may never learn of the details and are left simply to speculate on the extraordinary wealth their government officials have accumulated, purportedly on modest government salaries. This distinction often means that those countries talking about bribery the most—in the private sector, in the media and in the courts—hold the greatest promise for long-term transparency.

Consider a recent, highly publicized case of corruption in an established democracy. California Republican Congressman Randall "Duke" Cunningham tumbled from illustrious to indicted in just a few days. Cunningham was a decorated former Navy pilot who flew in Vietnam and later taught at the Navy's "Top Gun" school in Miramar, but it seems that his US$160,000 annual salary had begun to chafe. A member of the Defense Appropriations Subcommittee, Cunningham was well-placed to become a bit more entrepreneurial. He honed his bribery craft until his prices were documented in a 'bribe menu' written on his official stationary, complete with the congressional seal, that listed how much contractors would have to pay to buy multimillion-dollar government contracts.[82] He pleaded guilty to charges of bribery and tax evasion—bribe-takers rarely pay taxes on their bounty—on March 3, 2006.[83] In light of the previous chapter's discussion on gifts and favors in place of cash bribes, it should be noted that much of the money that flowed to Cunningham arose out of a reported "sweetheart" real estate deal rather than a direct payment of cash. Defense contractor Mitchell Wade purchased Cunningham's house at an inflated price of US$1,675,000 and then promptly put it back on the market; it sold after eight months with no activity for just US$975,000. The Criminal Information also states that Cunningham benefited from the use of a 42-foot yacht, first named the "Buoy Toy"—later renamed the "Duke-Stir"—and accepted an addition on his home, antiques and other furniture, and checks paid both directly to him and to his company, "Top Gun Enterprises, Inc."[84]

Typically, deals of this kind are difficult for enforcement agents to uncover. Most do not have the resources to track transactions of this kind, much less the wherewithal to investigate a transaction with no cooperating witnesses or undercover agents. In this case, the sale of the house was remarked upon in a local newspaper and the FBI opened an investigation that is still ongoing, with respect to additional participants, as of this writing.

What did this real estate deal buy Wade? A recent report indicates that Cunningham "used his post on the House Intelligence Committee to authorize more than $70 million in funding for projects sought by defense contractors who bribed him."[85] Cunningham was partying and living large and all the time "he was squandering precious tax dollars for, among other things, systems the military didn't ask for, didn't need and frequently didn't use," according to the Assistant U.S. Attorney handling the case.[86]

The Cunningham case is a further illustration of how corruption can siphon resources away from real national priorities. But it also illustrates how mature democracies can check corruption and correct the course of government. Not only were Cunningham's excesses widely exposed in the media, and not only was Cunningham himself successfully prosecuted for his crimes, but the American electorate also responded. Most analysts of the 2006 mid-term election in the United States concluded that the Cunningham case, and other political scandals that were in the news throughout 2005 and 2006, led to strong anti-incumbent sentiment in the electorate, resulting in a change in the majority party in both the U.S. Senate and the House of Representatives and a renewed focus on congressional ethics. This demonstrates the role an open media and competitive elections can play to elevate clean government as an element of campaign platforms.

The Political Potency of Corruption

Corruption has clear political potency, both for ill when it buys results that contradict the will of the electorate or is used as a smear tactic against those who would challenge the most powerful in society, and for reform when it generates outrage. The depressing record of bribers who have bought distorted, self-serving outcomes should not obscure the salutary results that follow when a free press vigorously investigates and exposes corrupt public figures and honest elections permit voters to fire corrupt officials.

The aforementioned case of Shanghai's Communist party chief was widely deemed by China-watchers to be a matter of political maneuvering. The official in question, Chen Liangyu, was a key player in the political faction headed by former President Jiang Zemin, and the charges against him were perceived as manifestations of President Hu Jintao's efforts to consolidate his own power.[87] None of this means that the charges were not valid, but it does mean that the country's institutional commitment to resisting corruption remains in question, despite such high profile cases.

Likewise, the former government in Nigeria, elected in part on an anti-bribery platform, soon hemorrhaged credibility. While discussing allegations of bribery is an important step toward greater transparency within the government, when the allegations reach the highest levels of government, the situation can be deemed irremediable. In September 2006, the Nigerian Senate was informed that the Economic and Financial Crimes Commission (EFCC) of Nigeria had thirty-one of the country's thirty-six state governors under investigation for corruption.[88] That same month, Vice President Abubakar was indicted by the EFCC for allegedly stealing campaign funds and for paying bribes and was later suspended by the ruling People's Democratic Party.[89] The appeals from Abubakar's indictment are ongoing, but that didn't prevent him from running for the presidency in 2007.

It is possible that the allegations against Abubakar were politically motivated, that they were raised by his boss, then President Obasanjo, who had vowed to prevent him from succeeding to the presidency.

For his part, Abubakar also accused Obasanjo of corruption.[90] It is possible that the allegations are partly or wholly true. What is certain,
however, is that the people of Nigeria know bribery to be rampant at
all levels of their government and know that it is likely to be used as a
tool for political ends just as it is a tool for self-enrichment. It is clear
that Nigeria has an endemic corruption problem at the highest levels
of government, and in the best possible case, confidence will grow only
with a great deal of time and demonstrated, consistent remedial steps.

Obasanjo kept his word as he left office; his party's candidate was
declared the winner of the April 21, 2007, election described by observ-
ers as a "charade."

Bartering from the Bench

Transparency and political will are not the only requirements for successfully ferreting out and combating corruption; one also needs a legal
system with enough integrity to see a prosecution through to its conclusion. That kind of system can be hard to come by. It is frightening to
contemplate a police force or military working against the interests of
public order and security, but in a thuggish entrepreneurial free-for-all,
it is at least as disturbing to think that the judiciary, the last and lofti-
est recourse to justice, cannot be trusted. There is something about the
black robes and polished wood that citizens want to trust—that they
want to find inspiring. But judges are not untainted by bribery.

In 2006, more than a dozen senior Chinese judges were arrested for
accepting bribes.[91] The Chief Justice of India has said that at least 20
percent of Indian judges are corrupt.[92] Forty-nine percent of all Filipino
lawyers claim to be aware of judges that are "on the take."[93] Bribe-taking
judges are compromising the rule of law in the criminal context, but
they are also making their countries less attractive for foreign investment. In one purely commercial case, an Indonesian lawyer asked for
sufficient funds from his U.S. corporate client to pay the judge for a
favorable decision in a contract dispute.[94] Needless to say, this gave the
client a whole new set of concerns about further investment in Indonesia; companies require confidence that the contracts they negotiate will
be upheld and enforced. Judges in civil law jurisdictions may be aided
in their quest for bribes by the longstanding custom of substantive *ex
parte* communications. Permitted, but strictly limited, in common law
jurisdictions, these private meetings between counsel and judges in the
absence of the other party are thought to facilitate negotiations for
bribes in the privacy and comfort of the judges' chambers.[95]

Determined judges in common law jurisdictions have nevertheless
developed bribery schemes of their own. Two judges in Mississippi
were found guilty in April 2007 of conspiring in a bribery scheme with
a local lawyer, Paul Minor, through which they received guaranteed

loans that were ultimately paid off for them by Minor. In exchange, the judges provided favorable rulings on Minor's lucrative personal injury cases.

In yet another example of creeping criminality, when one of the judges was investigated for misappropriation of state funds, Minor also paid his legal expenses and hired a public relations firm to assist him.[96]

LEGAL PRINCIPLES

In determining the duties of government officials, English law has long applied the quaintly named doctrine of "master and servant." The servant, in this case the government official, owes a duty of loyalty to the master that has hired him, in this case the public. The American equivalent is "honest services." The laws of the United States carry criminal penalties for honest services fraud that deprives a party of its representative's conscientious, loyal and unbiased service, free of deceit, undue influence, conflict of interest and self-enrichment.[97] Nothing is supposed to interfere with that professional duty, and certainly not schemes dedicated to self-enrichment.

But the reality is that the creativity and avarice of some government officials appear to be without limit. They buy votes and sell contracts; everything has a price. Bribes prevent the protection of scarce resources and interfere with programs addressing critical public health problems and urgent environmental challenges. Bribes skew democratic processes, the rule of law and national security, undermining the confidence of a country's citizens. Bribes undermine at their source both the quality and availability of the services that government officials are expected and paid to provide.

Legal principles governing the duty of loyalty that a public servant owes its "master," the citizenry, seem quaint next to generals who negotiate to subcontract their soldiers to the bad guys and doctors who extort payments in exchange for urgently needed and purportedly free medical treatment. The legitimacy and dignity of states deteriorate quickly when these principles fall by the wayside.

Chapter 5

Distorting Business

*That's right, my continental friends, we have spied on you because
you bribe. Your companies' products are often more costly, less
technically advanced or both, than your American competitors'.
As a result you bribe a lot.*

—James Woolsey, 1995, then CIA director, discussing allegations that
the U.S. intelligence services were electronically eavesdropping to
uncover bribery[1]

RISKY BUSINESS

Setting aside questions of business ethics and legality for a moment,
bribery is bad for business. Bribes increase the cost of doing business.
They are an additional, often unpredictable expense. It is difficult to
budget for bribes and bribes aren't tax deductible in the way that other
business expenses are.[2]

Bribes buy an unenforceable contract. A company that pays a bribe
to a government official in order to win business cannot enforce the
deal it has made. If a government official has made clear a willingness
to compromise his position of trust for a financial reward, it is difficult
to imagine that he won't violate the first company's trust if a second
company offers a larger sum. If the bribe-taking government official
leaves his position before the contract is awarded, the company must
begin negotiations again with his successor.

Bribes reward government officials who can deliver results. Often
this means delivering a shortcut through paper work or an end run
around regulations. The value of this kind of service only increases
as the number of administrative hurdles increases. This creates an
incentive for bribe-taking government officials to increase their value
to companies willing to pay bribes by increasing the bureaucracy surrounding the process. The more convoluted and opaque a procurement process becomes, the more dependent upon the corrupt official's
"assistance" a company grows.

A reputation for paying bribes can damage a company's business in-
country, and even unwitting association with bribe-payers can be risky.

General Electric (GE) faced a boycott of its products in Thailand after headlines there stated that GE was acquiring a company previously accused of bribery. In fact, GE had done everything right and cooperated fully with enforcement authorities to ensure the previous allegations were fully investigated.[3] Nonetheless, it suffered damage by association.

There is a significant "hassle factor" to bribery. Even if parties to a bribery scheme are willing to abuse their positions and violate the law, each bribe must nevertheless be negotiated. Negotiations can be time-consuming, and negotiations over a bribe are almost bound to be more time-consuming than most. Because negotiations for bribes must generally be conducted in stealth, there is the additional delay associated with determining who should be privy to the discussions, arranging clandestine meetings, and contriving the veiled language used to describe the transaction. Even after the bribe is arranged, agreed to, and delivered, there is the need to falsify records to account for the illicit transfer of company money from a corporate account either to cash or to the account, typically offshore, of the government official. This may be accompanied by the creation of false invoices that justify the payment; it may be accompanied by the creation of whole shell companies to mask the flow of money in ongoing bribe-tainted transactions. All of this is a lot of trouble, and it is likely to cause a lot more trouble.

Moreover, additional damage is done to a company's corporate culture. The payment of bribes is bound to nurture a corporate culture that places little value on respect for laws and good governance more generally. Employees are likely to find themselves embroiled in an increasing number of schemes as they first bribe, then misrepresent the fact with falsified records, then, when discovery seems imminent, try to destroy records and obstruct an investigation. The process becomes one long toboggan ride of malfeasance ending, in many cases, with enforcement action and reputational damage from which it is difficult to recover.

In spite of the risk and hassle associated with bribery, representatives of some companies nevertheless determine that it is simpler, or more efficient, or unavoidable to incorporate bribery into their business model. Because bribe-paying is risky for companies, the possibility of a bribe tends to be raised first by the government official seeking to enrich himself. This is true both in routine expediting payments—"if you pay a 'special fee,' I can have this done for you tomorrow"—and for commercial contracts—"I am happy to work with your company; your company always takes good care of me." Nevertheless, as discussed previously, an executive might make it easier for the government official by being too willing to hear the request or the executive might be selling a product that would not be competitive in a fair and untainted competition.

An image of corporate executives arriving in an impoverished country with briefcases full of cash and surveying the horizon for people to pay off still lingers. The truth, however, is that most companies blunder into bribery schemes and then don't know how to extricate themselves. An executive associated with a bribery scheme risks termination, involvement in a protracted and unpleasant investigation, personal fines, public humiliation, imprisonment, and in several countries, the death penalty.

Sound business principles should cause companies to avoid the legal and reputational risk and uncertainty associated with bribes—and many companies do. Those that choose to pay bribes argue that it simply isn't possible to do business successfully without paying them.[4] Examples of companies in this category range from those that crossed the line inadvertently, because the line is never perfectly clear, to those with spectacular criminal intent, often reflected in grand schemes of which bribery is just one small part. This chapter is about the schemes devised by those companies that do set out to pay government officials— whatever their motivation. It will address the close calls—corporate schemes that, while imaginative, may not shock the public—as well as the most egregious cases. In each, there was nevertheless a government official happy to compromise his own laws and to benefit at the expense of his countrymen, and in each, these companies made it easier for officials on the take.

COST OF COMMERCIAL BRIBERY

The commercial cost of bribery is not limited to the price that must be paid or even the opportunities that are lost because of bribes. When word got out that Titan's dubious payments in Benin might derail the Lockheed Martin deal, Titan's share price dropped 6 percent.[5] Lockheed's decision to abandon the deal resulted in a tumble of another 20 percent.[6] For the second quarter of 2005, Titan reported estimated costs of US$34.4 million in connection with its FCPA investigation and its terminated merger with Lockheed Martin Corp.[7] Although the share price had largely recovered by the time Titan found another buyer, the company is still reeling from the payment of one of the largest penalties assessed in the history of the U.S. anti-bribery law and multiple shareholder class action suits. According to the shareholders' lawyers, one class action was settled for US$61.5 million.[8] When Willbros Group Inc., an international construction and engineering contractor[9] active in Nigeria, announced on May 16, 2005, that violations of U.S. anti-bribery law could prevent the company from bidding on U.S. government contracts, share prices plummeted US$5.77, down 31 percent from the previous day's price of US$15.92.[10]

By comparison, BAE's share price shot up 6 percent when the British Serious Fraud Office announced suddenly that it was dropping its investigation into the Saudi contract, Al Yamamah.[11]

EXPENSIVE BRIBES: A LOOK AT ONE INDUSTRY

A previous chapter described doctors demanding bribes in exchange for purportedly free medical services, but the private sector provides particularly fertile ground for entrepreneurial doctors. In several countries, some or all of the medical community is employed by the state and, under most anti-bribery laws, any employee of the state is a government official. This means that many, perhaps most, of the doctors to whom pharmaceutical companies and medical device companies market in these countries are government officials with all of the legal implications that carries. These officials have enjoyed a long tradition of obeisance from major pharmaceutical companies.

In 2002, Syncor International Corporation, based in California, was a leading provider of high tech health services, including nuclear pharmacy services.[12] Syncor was active in Taiwan, through its subsidiary Syncor Taiwan Inc. According to facts cited in a 2002 complaint filed by the SEC,[13] Syncor Taiwan marketed its products to state-owned hospitals and state-owned medical imaging centers and operated its own medical imaging centers. The company appears to have set up a fairly organized payment scheme for government officials by which the doctors in charge of purchasing decisions for some hospitals were paid "commissions" of 10–20 percent on the equipment they ordered from Syncor Taiwan. The company also paid fees to doctors for referring patients to Syncor Taiwan's medical imaging centers. In these cases, the payments were typically 3–5 percent of the patients' bills at the center, paid in cash to the referring doctor. The practice of medical professionals buying equipment their facilities don't need—or paying inflated prices for equipment they do need—costs taxpayers directly, while also diverting funds needed for valid purchases and services. Creating financial incentives to send patients for expensive and elaborate treatment is even more worrying.

A little more than two years after Syncor Taiwan pleaded guilty to violating the FCPA, Micrus Corporation settled a matter with similar facts.[14] Micrus is another California company which develops and sells embolic coils for the treatment of aneurysms. In March 2005, Micrus admitted to paying more than US$105,000 to doctors at state hospitals in France, Turkey, Spain, and Germany in return for their decision to purchase Micrus products.[15] According to the U.S. Department of Justice, the payments were recorded on the books as "stock options, honorariums[sic] and commissions."[16] It is possible that these officials would have purchased these products from Micrus in any event. The same year DPC (Tianjin) Ltd., a wholly-owned Chinese subsidiary of Diagnostic Products Corporation, pleaded guilty to charges that they had paid US$1.6 million in "commissions" to doctors and lab personnel at state-owned hospitals in China.[17] The U.S. Department of Justice reported that the payments were made over eleven years and, typically, were between 3 and 10 percent of sales.[18] The payments were meant to provide an incentive to the doctors and their staff to buy DPC Tianjin's medical products. The company's profits from the sales are estimated at US$2 million. The Chinese government officials' profits rival those of the company that developed, manufactured, and sold the product.

When payments of this kind are made in a purely private sector context, they are inappropriate kickbacks. When the recipient is on the government payroll and bound to act in the interest of the public, they are a violation of the Foreign Corrupt Practices Act.

The nefarious nature of these payments can't have been lost on either the company representatives or those receiving the bribes. Both DPC Tianjin and Syncor Taiwan hand-delivered cash payments. DPC Tianjin's salespeople delivered that company's bribes and Syncor Taiwan's were delivered by the subsidiary's general manager—the brother of the parent company's founder and chairman. Syncor Taiwan called the payments "promotional expenses."[19] DPC Tianjin recorded the payments on the company's books as "selling expenses"[20] which is strangely accurate, if not sufficiently accurate in the minds of U.S. prosecutors.

Germany has had a rash of such cases of its own recently. Prosecutors in Munich are investigating alleged bribes paid by German subsidiaries of pharmaceutical giant Bristol-Myers Squibb. The SEC notified the company on October 4, 2006, that it too was jumping into the fray with a formal investigation of its own.[21] GlaxoSmithKline is also under investigation in Germany for allegations of bribery, including claims that their sales representatives gave at least 1,600 gifts to German doctors[22] and, on December 18, 2006, German investigators searched the homes of hundreds of Ratiopharm International sales representatives suspected of providing doctors with cash and gifts in exchange for prescribing Ratiopharm products.[23] Just as the initial waves of U.S. anti-bribery enforcement seemed to target the defense industry, the pharmaceutical industry seems to be the current industry of choice for European enforcers.

UNENFORCEABLE CONTRACTS: NO HONOR AMONGST THIEVES

The strange and shady deals these companies cut are often disavowed by government officials who take the money and then fail to deliver on their illicit promise. Products of the private sector, executives are used to negotiating favorable deals for themselves and turning to their counsel when things don't work out, so it can be frustrating to realize that the laws that enable parties to negotiate contracts with confidence play no role in the world of bribery. Nevertheless, it is easy to imagine legions of well-placed individuals selling access they don't actually have and trading on exaggerated procurement authority. It is easier still to imagine the need to enforce some provision of a contract when the contract was, at its outset, illegal.

World Duty Free Company Limited (World Duty Free) submitted just such a dispute to arbitration on June 16, 2000.[24] In 1989, World Duty Free entered into a contract to construct, maintain, and operate duty-free complexes at Nairobi and Mombassa International Airports under a ten year lease, with an option to renew. The owner of World Duty Free claimed that, in order to do business with the government of Kenya, he was required to make a US$2 million cash "personal donation" to then President Moi.[25] Upon securing the contract, World Duty Free spent a reported US$27 million on airport improvements. World Duty Free claimed in arbitration that the government of Kenya was in breach of the contract and sought a variety of remedies. The government of Kenya argued that, because the contract was obtained by bribery—the US$2 million given to their own president—it was unenforceable as a matter of law and public policy. The arbitral tribunal agreed with the government of Kenya, stating that World Duty Free could not proceed with its claims as a matter of international public policy and applicable local law.[26]

There often is a legal gray area between the time when state resources are firmly within the control of the government and the time when they are truly owned by the public through the privatization process. During this transition, there are often opportunities for bold entrepreneurs unconstrained by strict business ethics to pay government officials to rig the process in their favor. More than one newly-minted billionaire has made his fortune this way. Viktor Kozeny, the "Pirate of Prague" discussed in Chapter 3 is alleged to have paid more than US$11 million to government officials in Azerbaijan in 1998 to gain control of the State Oil Company of Azerbaijan Republic during the privatization process.[27] Kozeny's company, the aptly named "Oily Rock Group" is reported to have promised individual Azeri officials two-thirds of the profits associated with the company's investment.[28] If successful, the scheme as described would have neatly transferred control of Azerbaijan's substantial oil resources from the government to Kozeny and a handful of individual government officials—theft on a truly grand scale. Soon after news of the scheme broke, however, reports surfaced that Kozeny may also have worked to cut his shifty government partners out of the deal.

It is not always the companies who are "victims" of promises not delivered. There are other examples of government officials who find themselves on the wrong end of an unenforceable deal. Equatorial Guinea is among the smallest countries in Africa, but it is that continent's third largest oil producer.[29] Like so many oil-rich nations, it should be more prosperous than it is. Instead, Equatorial Guinea has a

30 percent unemployment rate, struggles with cholera due to contaminated drinking water and has an average life expectancy of just forty-nine years. The same size as Maryland, but with a population of just over half a million people, the country is misgoverned to an extraordinary extent by its military regime. President Obiang has declared oil revenues to be a "state secret," but we know from the Riggs Bank scandal that at least US$700 million was squirreled away in private Obiang accounts in Washington. Equatorial Guinea is not, in short, a model of good government, but it controls oil fields containing at least 600 million barrels.

One government official in Malabo commented on the large and growing presence of Chinese companies in Equatorial Guinea.[30] The Chinese embassy is a vast block of a building on an island with few paved roads and a single-story open-air university smaller than an average high school. The Chinese are doing well in Equatorial Guinea. Too well, it seems. Some Chinese businessmen reportedly arrive ready to promise whatever it takes to win contracts. As the official's story unfolded, however, it became clear that follow-through on these promises is inconsistent. Some Chinese businessmen operating in Equatorial Guinea have developed a reputation for reneging on promises of elaborate gifts and travel and, in some cases, cash for government officials. Once the official deal is reduced to writing, the illicit side deals are forgotten. Equatoguinean government officials once so well-disposed to their generous suitors are left with a less favorable contract than they might have been able to negotiate if self-interest hadn't intervened and they had dealt openly and honestly. It is to the government officials' credit that they're able to see the irony in this. One remarked, "We are better off dealing with the Americans. They aren't generous, but we know what we're getting." In far-flung bribery circles, it seems, anyone can become a victim, although some victims invoke less sympathy than others.

CORRUPTION QUAGMIRE

When companies set out to pursue business in countries with little commercial transparency, the bribes tend to start early in the process. It is unlikely that a company can reach the final stages of a large contract without facing demands from junior officials along the way. The corrupt machinery that supports senior bribe-taking officials is typically stoked by a much larger number of grasping junior officials at the bottom, but ambitious to work their way up. This can have a deadening effect on business in countries already struggling to attract foreign investment. When officials on each rung of the ladder insist on a cut of the ultimate profit, expense and uncertainty increase, and productivity decreases.

ABB Ltd. is a Zurich-based group of companies in the field of power and automation technologies with operations in over 100 countries. ABB "enable[s] utility and industry customers to improve performance while lowering environment impact."[31] Until 2004, ABB Vetco Gray Inc. and ABB Vetco Gray UK Ltd. were subsidiaries of the Swiss parent and were based in Houston and Aberdeen respectively. In July 2004, the two subsidiaries pleaded guilty to two counts of bribery before a federal judge in Houston. Both companies admitted that they had paid more than US$1 million to officials working at the National Petroleum Investment Management Services (NAPIMS), a Nigerian government agency, in order to gain access to confidential bid information.[32] The companies also admitted to providing government officials with gifts, lavish hospitality, travel and, for their wives, surprisingly, pedicures. NAPIMS is an influential agency;[33] it approves bidders seeking to work on oil exploration projects in Nigeria, including those seeking to work as contractors to foreign companies already operating in Nigeria. NAPIMS holds, in effect, the keys to all oil and gas contracts in Nigeria. The ABB subsidiaries' payments were also designed to secure NAPIMS recommendations with respect to seven construction contracts in-country, for which profits were estimated to be almost US$12 million.[34] Over US$1 million in bribes to realize a possible profit of US$12 million is a considerable tax on doing business in Nigeria—a tax that flows not to the citizens of Nigeria, but to a handful of government officials. Each of the two subsidiaries agreed to pay a fine of US$5.25 million and the parent, ABB Ltd., agreed to pay an additional US$5.9 million to settle these and other allegations with the SEC. In a separate proceeding in July 2006, four senior ABB executives individually settled enforcement actions with the SEC and agreed to civil monetary judgments ranging from US$40,000 to US$50,000 each.[35]

Three Vetco International Ltd. subsidiaries pleaded guilty on February 2, 2007, to subsequent violations of the FCPA. Nigeria was at the center of this scandal, too. Allegations of 378 corrupt payments totaling approximately US$2.1 million to Nigerian Customs Service officials resulted in fines for the three subsidiaries that totaled US$26 million.[36]

There is another Nigerian oil and gas bribery scandal that is reportedly under investigation in five countries.[37] The story begins—during Abacha's heyday—on Bonny Island, a small community in the Niger Delta off the coast of Nigeria. The indigenous Ibani people have long been part of a traditional, fishing community, overshadowed for a time in the nineteenth century when the island was the leading site in West Africa for the export of slaves. The island attracted attention again in the 1960s when the updated port became a key export site for petroleum refined at Port Harcourt. Today, the island is relatively peaceful, although heavily polluted from the influx of heavy industry.[38]

In 1994, M.W. Kellogg, a London-based company, entered into a joint venture partnership with three other entities: Technip in France, JGC Corporation in Japan, and Snamprogetti, a subsidiary of ENI SpA in Italy. M.W. Kellogg is now part of KBR, a division of Halliburton. Using the initials from each owner, the joint venture was called TSKJ and it bid successfully on a contract to build a liquefied natural gas plant in Nigeria. The joint venture then hired Jeffrey Tesler, a London lawyer with no apparent oil and gas experience, to help it win additional business in Nigeria. The choice struck many in the industry as a bit peculiar, but success followed. In 1999, TSKJ won a second contract worth US$1.4 billion for construction at the same Bonny Island complex. Less than two weeks after the second contract was awarded, TSKJ signed a contract with Tri-Star, a company Jeffrey Tesler set up in Gibraltar, agreeing to pay Tri-Star US$37.5 million. The total paid to Tesler by the joint venture is reported to exceed US$180 million for a man who has spent, to date, just eight hours on the ground in Nigeria. Approximately US$100 million of this has been frozen by the Swiss authorities, pending an investigation.

The allegedly crooked deal began to unravel in 2002 when Georges Krammer, a former executive with the joint venture's French partner, Technip, told a French investigating judge that the joint venture established a US$175 million "slush fund" to bribe Nigerian officials.[39]

In October 2006, Halliburton disclosed to the SEC that three people have been dismissed in the wake of their internal investigation into improper payments, but Halliburton has acknowledged that some representatives involved in the alleged payment scheme continue to work for the company.[40] The allegations, as they stand now, are that TSKJ paid Jeffrey Tesler US$180 million both for his services and as discretionary funds for inappropriate payments to Nigerian officials. Some of this money is alleged to have made its way back to corporate executives and the final destination of the balance remains unclear.

Halliburton dismissed Albert ("Jack") Stanley, a former CEO of KBR, in 2004 after determining that he received what they called "improper personal benefits"—and what reporters have called a 5 percent kickback—from Tesler.[41] Even well-paid corporate executives can be tempted by the millions of dollars that change hands in large international contracts. For executives already operating outside the bounds of good corporate governance, it probably is easier to step over the final line and, in the end, to ensure that they cash in themselves. After years of operating in this climate, the financial sleight of hand made possible by shell companies and numbered off-shore accounts is often well-practiced.

More recently, representatives of TSKJ are alleged to have paid US$2.4 million to Nigerian tax officials for a more "favorable" tax assessment in that country.[42] Bribes to reduce taxes on profits from contracts won by bribery seems at least one theft too many.

MORE PARTIES, MORE RISK

Many bribes are conveyed to their ultimate recipients indirectly through trusted third parties rather than being made directly to a lofty government official. A more direct approach can seem a bit tactless and an intermediary can smooth the way like a good matchmaker. These intermediaries might be sales agents, consultants, or the business advisors discussed previously. When this approach to marketing is above-board, commercial intermediaries can provide legitimate access and help build relationships with key decision-makers. They can help companies explore business opportunities in new markets and navigate language and cultural obstacles without the expense and risk of establishing a presence in-country. When commercial intermediaries become a vector for bribes—with a company's knowledge or unwittingly—their involvement can be both efficient and difficult to detect. Intermediaries are often able to act in stealth precisely because they understand the local market.

Costa Rica has a strangely clean reputation for a country whose last three presidents have been accused of bribery, but the French telecommunications giant, Alcatel, has been mired in scandal in this prosperous Central American state for years. Indeed, two of the three presidents under suspicion for bribery have been connected to the Alcatel scandal. There are over a million cellular phones for the four million inhabitants of Costa Rica,[43] so cellular telephone contracts are big business. Prior to 2001, Alcatel struggled to break into the market, but repeatedly lost to a competitor with different technology. Beginning in 2000, Alcatel reportedly set out to slant the playing field their way. According to allegations made by both the Costa Rican government and the U.S. Department of Justice, Alcatel worked through a local Costa Rican consulting firm to make payments to an official with the state-owned telecommunications authority. In exchange for these payments, the official was expected "to exercise his influence to initiate a bid process which favored Alcatel's technology and to vote to award Alcatel a mobile telephone contract."[44]

Alcatel was working the intermediary device with considerable skill, but there are refinements they could learn. Titan managed to reach higher in the decision-making process when it paid more than US$2 million to its agent in Benin who was also known to be the business advisor of the then-incumbent president of Benin. When a rogue Monsanto employee wanted to bribe an Indonesian government official, he turned to a local consulting firm. When ABB wanted to pay bribes to officials of Nigeria's state-owned NAPIMS in exchange for confidential bid information and favorable consideration for contracts, the employees channeled the money through a consultant and disguised the payments as fees for consulting work.[45] In keeping with the "slippery slope" theme, one ABB employee is alleged to have then negotiated a US$50,000 kickback from a NAPIMS official, thereby working both ends of the deal.[46] It is not clear whether the vocabulary of corruption has a reliable term for a kickback on a bribe.

BellSouth International raised the use of commercial intermediaries to an art form in Nicaragua. In the latter part of the 1990s, BellSouth sought to increase its ownership of Telefonia Celular de Nicaragua, S.A. (Telefonia), a Nicaraguan telecommunications company. Nicaraguan law, however, prevented foreign ownership of a majority interest in Nicaraguan telecommunications companies—a practice many countries follow on national security grounds. BellSouth was at a standstill. In 1998, BellSouth retained a businesswoman to provide lobbying support for the repeal of the foreign ownership restriction. The intermediary they selected and paid handsomely had no prior lobbying experience, but her compensation package was the second most lucrative within Telefonia. She was well-connected. She was married to the Chair of the Nicaraguan legislative committee with oversight authority for telecommunications. During the course of this commercial relationship, the husband drafted legislation proposing the repeal of the foreign ownership restriction, garnered committee support and scheduled and presided over the hearings at which arguments from BellSouth and others were heard.

In December 1999, the National Assembly accepted the Committee's recommendation and repealed the restriction. Six months later, BellSouth exercised its option and became the majority owner of Telefonia.[47] On January 15, 2002, BellSouth settled with the SEC for its role in this matter and paid a civil penalty of US$150,000.

Bribe-conveying third party intermediaries can take other forms, too. While sales representatives and consultants are the usual conduits, law firms[48] and accountants are often well-positioned not only to make illicit payments for their clients, but to bury them in the large and often vague bills they routinely generate.

Baker Hughes is an oil field services company based in Houston and active in over 90 countries.[49] In September 2001, the SEC and Department of Justice, acting jointly, settled allegations of bribery with Baker Hughes arising out of the activities of its Indonesian subsidiary, PT Eastman Christiensen (PTEC). According to the SEC account of the matter,[50] PTEC had filed tax returns and was awaiting what it expected would be a hefty refund. Instead of a refund, PTEC was notified that the company's 1997 tax return would be audited. The audit resulted in a tax bill, clearly inflated, totaling US$3.2 million. Shortly after the tax bill was delivered, an Indonesian government official stepped forward and offered to reduce the bill, for a US$200,000 fee. PTEC's local tax advisors, KPMG Siddharta Siddharta & Harsono (SS&H), an affiliate of the Swiss accounting giant, KPMG International, rejected the demand and recommended challenging the tax bill through official channels. Presumably seeking to accommodate an important client, however, SS&H also made it clear that, if Baker Hughes wanted to make the payment, the firm could generate a false accounting invoice to cover the cost.

Growing impatient, the Indonesian tax official offered, as a part of the deal, to reduce his demand to US$75,000 and sweetened the deal by offering to reduce the inflated tax bill of US$3.2 million to just US$270,000. According to the official, the matter could be resolved with this payment, or the company could pay the full assessment and take its chances in a protracted appeal of the decision. The official gave PTEC just 48 hours to decide. At this point, the Baker Hughes' regional tax manager, based in Australia, lobbed the matter to Houston. The response from Baker Hughes' senior manager, in concert with the company's outside counsel, provides a brief case study for good governance: the parent company's General Counsel sent a clear and emphatic message that no payment was to be made either directly or through the accounting firm.

Later that day, the company's Chief Financial Officer (CFO), who had been present for the meeting with the company's lawyers, instructed his regional tax manager to proceed with the payment anyway and to have SS&H record the payment as a "success fee." Acting on the CFO's instructions, SS&H made the payment and billed the company as instructed and PTEC received the promised tax assessment of US$270,000.

As soon as Baker Hughes' General Counsel learned that the payment had been authorized, the company took immediate action to undo the damage and cooperated with the U.S. Department of Justice, which publicly acknowledged the company's assistance. Successful bribetakers have to be able to communicate their demands to their target. In this case, it was simpler for the tax official to work initially through the local accounting firm. In addition, once the General Counsel had rejected the proposed bribe, it was only with the help of their intermediary, in this case SS&H, that the CFO and the regional tax manager were able to collaborate and ensure the illegal payment was made and the books and records falsified.

In another case involving one apparently ardent intermediary, the representative of a Canadian company is suing U.S. defense giant Lockheed Martin on the grounds that the latter's intermediary won business by bribing the then South Korean defense minister with "sexual favors."[51] The former defense minister, Lee Yang Ho, admitted to having a relationship with Lockheed Martin's commercial intermediary, Ms. Linda Kim, but claimed that his procurement decisions in Lockheed's favor were not influenced by the relationship.

It is more difficult to do business in countries with rampant bribery. Employees based overseas must navigate their way through bribes which often begin as soon as they land, with airport and customs officials, and continue throughout their stay. Extortionate demands may arise in connection with personal services; bribes may be demanded for everything from telephone service and drivers' licenses to emergency evacuation for urgent medical care. This is in addition to the bribe demands that may be faced at the office.

For corporate employees back at headquarters, there are challenges to be navigated and these can be complicated by commercial intermediaries, even when working with reputable local representatives overseas. These commercial intermediaries can offer local expertise and surprising insight not readily available to an expatriate. One company trying to penetrate a difficult market in Pakistan retained such a local representative and the parties agreed that he should be paid on a commission—6 percent of every sale he was able to facilitate in-country. Pakistani law prohibits its citizens from being paid outside Pakistan for work undertaken inside the country. Many countries have similar laws in order to reduce black market currency exchanges and to ensure access to tax revenue. The company and the intermediary determined that the requirements of the law would be satisfied if the company paid by check, to be mailed directly to the agent in Pakistan. Sales were strong and the partnership flourished until the agent contacted the company and indicated that the arrangements for payment they had structured were no longer viable. The agent was reluctant to explain the problem initially.

It turned out that each commission check was being opened by someone within the Pakistani postal system. The checks were sent in slim envelopes and there can have been no concern that anything other than paperwork was contained within. The official within the post office would then send a postal carrier to the intermediary's office, together with a menacing armed guard. The two would invite the intermediary to accompany them to his bank where he was expected to cash the check and give them a hefty share of it. The more successful the intermediary became, the more attention his mail received, until he determined it was no longer viable for him to continue.[52]

Government officials often have unique access to sensitive or proprietary information and many are prepared to turn this information to their advantage. This presents logistical challenges for employees of multinational companies who must not only invest the time to find practical solutions to problems of this kind, but must protect those associated with their company from risks that arise precisely because the company is seen as a rich source of bribes.

More measurable than these very real practical challenges, though, is the cost to a country in lost foreign direct investment. In one study, representatives of the World Bank demonstrated convincingly that poor governance and rampant bribery results in a tax on foreign direct investment as high as 15 percent in countries like Mexico. Not only are foreign officials increasing costs to business and to their countrymen by skimming from contracts through bribes and then shipping their ill-gotten profits off-shore, but their behavior, collectively, is discouraging future investment in their country.[53] Though it is difficult to quantify the investment foregone in this way, this may be the single greatest cost inflicted on a country by the greed of its officials. Petty graft may have immense consequences as investors put a country on the "too hard to do business" list, or simply bypass it because similar opportunities exist in countries where they can be confident that the bribe-driven hassle factor will be less pronounced.

A CORPORATE CULTURE OF MALFEASANCE

The connection between bribery and poor corporate governance was best established by the prosecution of the Elf Aquitaine case in France in 2003. The Elf case is often trumpeted as the first major anti-bribery prosecution in France. The title doesn't quite fit, however, as the eight-year investigation and four-month trial uncovered bribes paid well before transnational bribery was made a crime in France,[54] an event which didn't occur until June of 2000. The investigation established that Elf had set-up a slush fund from which bribes were to be paid, sending the clear message that company funds could be used to buy a business advantage both within France and abroad. The money wasn't always spent for the intended purpose, however. Senior company officials, including the CEO of the company, Loik Le Floch-Prigent, and Elf's "Mr. Africa," Mr. Andre Tarallo, helped themselves to hundreds of millions of dollars from the account established to bribe foreign government officials. Before the trials were over there were tales of embezzlement, bribery on a massive scale, and courtesans hired to suborn French government ministers.[55] It appears that there is considerable temptation to obscure the boundaries of criminality once executives start down that path.

Elf was later purchased by Total. Several Total executives are currently under investigation in France for paying bribes to foreign officials and for allegations of inappropriate business practices arising out of the United Nations Oil-for-Food Program.[56]

The story of Saint Regis University illustrates the potential layers of malfeasance and harm that a single bribery scheme can entail. Saint Regis should not be confused with Regis College in Weston, Massachusetts, or Regis University in Denver, Colorado, both of which have, for example, buildings and books. Saint Regis, by comparison, is a "virtual university" named after a French saint revered for taking pity on the uneducated. It is a university for people who don't really want to go to university. Saint Regis is a "diploma mill."[57] In exchange for a fee and "life experience," a customer can obtain a Master's degree from Saint Regis through the mail. Saint Regis isn't the only diploma mill and the story wouldn't be very interesting if it ended there. Apparently determined to rise above its diploma mill status, the owners, Dixie and Stephen Randock, set out to buy some legitimacy.

Working through Richard Novak, who holds three doctoral degrees from the illustrious Saint Regis, the University approached the Liberian embassy in Washington with plans for accreditation. Liberia is not a country rich in universities. This West African country has suffered through two civil wars in the last twenty years which, together, destroyed the economy of this resource-rich country. Educational goals were pushed aside by the extraordinary violence perpetrated in part by the legions of child soldiers recruited by the army until fewer than 18 percent of secondary school aged children were enrolled in school. In short, it is not clear that a university degree from Liberia would be an impressive centerpiece for a job-seeker's resume.

According to Novak's plea agreement,[58] the Liberian consul, unnamed in the documents and largely immune from prosecution because of his diplomatic status, offered to secure the necessary paperwork from his commissioner of higher education in exchange for US$4,000. When the "university" announced its accreditation, the Liberian embassy began receiving calls from potential customers. Dixie Randock is alleged to have then agreed to pay the Liberian consul US$400 per month to handle these calls and to speak to "the legitimacy of Saint Regis University."[59] Novak pleaded guilty to delivering these payments, including one that was filmed by the Secret Service in a Washington, D.C., hotel.

Before it was closed down, Saint Regis University had collected more than US$4 million from "students" eager to own the best degree they could buy. In addition, careless employers were probably impressed by these bogus credentials. Roughly half of the phony degrees were sent overseas where some probably were used to meet immigration requirements, raising concerns that they were used to falsely bolster visa applications for those seeking entry into a country for nefarious purposes.[60]

Commercial bribery transactions are replicated thousands of times over worldwide. Bribe schemes no doubt bring quick, short term cash to the people who perpetrate them, but it should be clear that the damage that commercial bribery does to a company is costly and far-reaching. Bribe-tainted deals are risky and uncertain. They create disreputable partnerships with unreliable partners. They mark corporations as easy targets, leading to more and greater demands from government officials who prefer reliable sources of bribes to uncertain possible new sources. They often result in additional financial crimes as the source, purpose and recipient of funds must be disguised. All of this is in addition to the large and growing fines and prison sentences and reputational damage companies suffer amongst shareholders and customers. If bribery is the only way a company can prevail in a market—if either the product is inferior or the price is too high—it may be wise for the company to reconsider its business model before it heads down a path of bribery, fraud and reputational risk.

Chapter 6

International Embarrassment

The United Nations lacks the capacity, controls, flexibility, robustness and indeed transparency to handle multibillion-dollar global operations.

—Former Secretary General Kofi Annan

BRIBERY ON A GLOBAL SCALE

Initiatives supported by a number of countries offer opportunities for corruption even richer than those undertaken by a single state or a single corporation. They often involve large sums; they generally fall into an indistinct region of the law where no single state's statutes apply with controlling force; they tend to take place in a politically charged atmosphere where candid language must be avoided and they frequently feature figures of considerable prestige and grand reputation. The international bureaucracies charged with directing or supervising these initiatives often move ponderously slowly, and never more slowly than when they are meant to be policing themselves. In such cases it is hardly necessary that the system break down in some way. When it works exactly as designed it practically broadcasts invitations to bribery and embezzlement.

THE UNITED NATIONS OIL-FOR-FOOD PROGRAM

There are few international organizations as controversial as the United Nations (UN). Founded in 1945, the UN provided a model by which countries could address transnational challenges, whether political, social, cultural, or humanitarian. To this end, the UN has developed some innovative and successful programs alongside some that undermined both the program's purpose and the reputation of the institution. The United Nations Oil-for-Food Program stands alone in terms of the breadth and scope of the corruption it unleashed. It provides a sad and powerful example of just how completely good intentions may be derailed and overtaken by those who celebrate greed.[1]

In August 1990, Iraq invaded Kuwait. Kuwait was subsequently lib-
erated by coalition forces in February 1991. As a result, the Security
Council passed United Nations Resolution 687, imposing onerous
sanctions on Iraq that continued for five years, through January 1996.
During sanctions, most trade and financial transactions were prohibited with Iraq and the country received no humanitarian assistance.
Sanctions would not be lifted unless and until then Iraqi president
Saddam Hussein complied with the Security Council's requirements
for cooperation with international weapons inspections and disarma-
ment. For five years, the Iraqi leadership[2] fought to have the sanctions
lifted. Trade could resume only after weapons inspectors were assured
that the country was fully disarmed of any weapons of mass destruc-
tion: long-range missiles, chemical weapons, and biological weapons.[3]

As early as 1991, the UN sought to authorize the limited sale of oil
in return for the purchase of food and medicine for the Iraqi people, but
these efforts were rejected by the Iraqi leadership. Under such a program, the Iraqi government would be permitted to sell small amounts
of its oil, under carefully controlled conditions. The proceeds would be
managed by the UN and used solely to buy food and medicine for the
people of Iraq. With such a program, the UN was moving into uncharted
territory where it would essentially administer the oil sales of the country of Iraq, a role for which it gave no evidence of being equipped.

On May 20, 1996, the Iraqi leadership finally agreed to enter into
a Memorandum of Understanding (MOU) with the United Nations,
authorizing what became know as the UN Oil-for-Food Program's ("the
Program"). In order to implement the Program, the UN established the
Office of Iraqi Programs, with Mr. Benon Sevan as the Executive Director responsible for the Program's administration from its beginning in
October 1991 until the Program's end in 2003. What began as a 180-
day temporary humanitarian relief program ultimately stretched into
a seven-year program with US$100 billion dollars in transactions. The
"humanitarian aid" in the form of food and medicine that the UN was
anxious to get to the people of Iraq expanded over time to include the
construction of port facilities, highways, sports stadiums, and, many
suspect, armaments.

The UN's goal was to expedite relief to the Iraqis without even the
modest delay that basic good governance, limited oversight, and mini-
mal record-keeping controls required. Saddam Hussein's exploitation
of the Program by diverting funds to himself and others outside of the
Program's processes together with a lack of sufficient UN controls, corporations and individuals willing to participate in the scheme, and the
absence of any rule of law in Iraq, created a virtual pipeline through
which money could easily be diverted to nefarious ends.

What went wrong? Perhaps one of the greatest flaws of the Program
was embedded in the MOU itself. In a nod to Iraqi sovereignty, the UN

determined that Iraq should be free to select the customers to whom the Iraqis would sell their oil as well as the companies from which Iraq would purchase humanitarian supplies with the oil proceeds. Through the escrow account, the UN collected the oil proceeds and from those proceeds paid the humanitarian suppliers. As designed, the Program provided Saddam Hussein with the freedom and the ability to demand 'side payments,' bribes, and kickbacks from the oil purchasers and humanitarian suppliers if they wanted to receive lucrative contracts from Iraq. Over time, Saddam Hussein realized the opportunities for additional income and imposed what can only be characterized as 'state mandated' corruption where the oil purchasers and humanitarian suppliers had to "pay to play." What the world saw was a secure UN bank managing huge sums for the good of the Iraqi people. What the world could not see was Saddam Hussein, parked up the street, collecting tolls from those who wanted lucrative contracts under the Program.

Because Saddam Hussein could decide who was permitted to buy Iraqi oil, he was able to use it to his political advantage. The UN made this easier by permitting the Iraqi leadership to set the price at which the oil could be sold, providing Hussein with additional leverage. He sold the oil at below-market prices to countries—and later individuals—willing to lean his way on the UN Security Council. Growing more sophisticated over time, he began to contact potential buyers surreptitiously. He advised them that they would have to agree to pay a "surcharge" of between US$0.10 and US$0.50 per barrel before he would allocate oil to them. Again, this was made easier by the reduced price; even with the surcharge, the price per barrel was attractive to buyers. The illegal oil surcharges that began in August 2000—bribes to Hussein in return for lucrative oil contracts—were paid directly or through front companies and occasionally in bags of cash delivered to Iraqi embassies.[4] The Iraqi leadership collected US$229 million in oil surcharges before the UN caught on, warned companies that paying the surcharge was a violation of sanctions, and put an end to it.

Around the same time that Iraq began requesting the payment of oil surcharges, Iraqi ministries were ordered to collect kickbacks on all contracts with humanitarian suppliers. These kickbacks were paid by willing companies in the form of "inland transportation fees" or "after sales service fees" and totaled US$1.6 billion. This was corruption on a far grander scale than the oil surcharges. Those wishing to sell to Iraq had to pay these fees directly to Iraq, often as part of a written "side agreement" that the UN never saw. Of course, the illegal side payments never made their way into the UN escrow account, but instead lined the pockets of Saddam Hussein and his cronies.

The inland transportation fees, officially designed to cover the cost of transportation by truck from the Iraqi port of Umm Qasr and other points of entry, bore no relation to the modest transportation costs reflected in previous transactions. This was simply another surcharge, another way for Saddam Hussein to subvert funds from the Program into his own coffers. The scale, however, was quite grand. In 2001, Iraq was paying US$25 per metric ton of rice. Just one year later, Iraq was paying more than twice that: US$59 per metric ton. The international rice market hadn't changed at all from 2001 to 2002, but the cost of "inland transportation" had escalated. A program designed to ensure that the oil wealth of Iraq was used to ensure food and medicine for the people of Iraq was quickly manipulated to ensure that companies and, more dramatically, those in power in Iraq, were benefiting from the revenue. The inflated prices cost companies nothing. They were encouraged to simply pass the cost through to the UN escrow account. Companies were practically invited to inflate their prices in exchange for ensuring that Hussein got his cut. Market forces had no role to play in this strange program because neither the buyer, Saddam Hussein, nor the sellers had the interests of the ultimate consumers, the people of Iraq, in mind. When the rice finally hit the markets of Baghdad, the consumers were left to bear the inflated price—the companies had what they wanted and Hussein had what he wanted.

Together, these kickback schemes are thought to have netted Hussein about US$1.6 billion, although ongoing investigations indicate that the number may be much higher.[5] Hussein, apparently aware of the slippery slope syndrome, required those associated with the program to keep meticulous records of the bribes paid and falsely recorded as inland transportation fees. Presumably, he feared the Elf factor—the possibility that his subordinates, when faced with millions of dollars of illicit income would be tempted to help themselves.

Iraqis reportedly knew that the Oil-for-Food Program was being mocked and abused by the Iraqi regime. The sanctions were devastating for ordinary Iraqis and the Oil-for-Food largesse a boon to very few. It is difficult to imagine what long-term damage the Oil-for-Food Program did to the Iraqi people's confidence in the international community and in the ability of international organizations to provide effective humanitarian assistance. Beyond that, we have seen the longer term and perhaps enduring damage that the Program has caused to the reputation of the UN and its ability to garner support for future humanitarian initiatives on this scale.

The Program itself was flawed and its implementation marred by weak control and ineffective oversight. The role of one individual deserves special mention. The Office of Iraqi Programs, mentioned previously, was directed by Mr. Benon Sevan. Sevan rose to the level of Under-Secretary-General and remained the UN's principal officer in charge of administering the Oil-for-Food Program. What was not learned until long after the Program ended was that Under-Secretary-General Sevan not only concealed Iraqi abuses of the Program from his superiors at the UN, but that he also was designated by Iraqi leadership as a beneficiary of Iraqi allocations of oil. That is, the chief administrator of the sanctions program was one of the individuals singled out as an ally of Saddam Hussein's cause and financially rewarded for his role. Although Sevan has been indicted by a U.S. court, he remains in his native Cyprus, beyond the reach of that court due to the absence of a treaty between the two countries that would compel his return to the U.S. to stand trial. Before returning to Cyprus, Sevan gave this erudite response to negative media accounts of the situation on CNN News: "You tell me, we are scheming– scheming what? What proof do you have to scheme anything? I'm very sorry to say. It's very easy to talk. La, la, la, la. You know?"[6]

The international community was startled not only by the scope and creativity of the Iraqi regime's abuses of the Oil-for-Food Program, but also by the international business community's complicity. On the oil side, 138 companies paid US$229 million in illegal surcharges to Iraq,[7] while humanitarian aid suppliers paid kickbacks of approximately US$1.6 billion.[8] Iraq was, by then, an international pariah and Saddam Hussein was convincingly implicated in genocide, but companies apparently paid because it was the cost of doing business—because they believed they had no alternative if they wanted access to the lucrative contracts that Saddam Hussein could guarantee.

In Australia, a public inquiry has been conducted into the involvement of the Australian Wheat Board. In December 2006, the Cole Inquiry concluded that the Australian Wheat Board paid US$220 million in bribes to secure contracts valued at US$2.3 billion,[9] aligning neatly with assertions that the Iraqi regime pocketed about 10 percent of all commerce throughout the Oil-for-Food Program. The inquiry concluded with a recommendation that eleven executives of the Australian Wheat Board should face criminal charges for their involvement in the bribery scheme. The Australian government has, at least, investigated. While 26 countries have requested and received assistance from the Independent Inquiry Committee established to investigate the Program, many others have taken no action. Russia and China, both very active in Iraq during the period of the sanctions, haven't even bothered to make a gesture toward enforcement for the sake of appearances.[10]

French oil company Total SA has been carefully scrutinized for its role in the Oil-for-Food Program but with a very different corporate response to date. Christophe de Margerie, the former head of Total's exploration and production division, was taken into custody and charged in October 2006 in relation to allegedly illegal payments under the Program.[11] That matter is currently pending, but the company's surprising response was to elevate de Margerie to CEO just four months later in early 2007.[12]

Several European companies seem to be dodging the enforcement bullet. Swiss inspections company, Cotecna, was retained by the Oil-for-Food Program to inspect and process shipments into Iraq. There was early interest in Cotecna because of its link with Secretary General Kofi Annan through his son, Kojo Annan, a long-standing employee. That interest appears to have fizzled initially, but was revived when German authorities alleged that DaimlerChrysler bribed Cotecna to process its shipments into Iraq ahead of others. It is challenging to find any transaction radiating out from Iraq during this period that is not tainted by allegations of bribery.

The international community looks on while the UN imposes sanctions that are ineffective, causing hardship for many and bringing great profit to those they are meant to punish. The international business community pays what is asked of it, confident that there will be little oversight from the UN and none from their own countries. The chief enforcer takes his cut and retires to Cyprus. The whole system starts to look as though it was designed more to facilitate than to deter bribery. A final legal dilemma sums it all up: the Iraqi regime used the program to steal from itself. Several commentators have stated that there is no clear victim, which must come as a surprise to Iraqi citizens who watched the UN escrow account depleted, observed the empty shelves at markets and saw the new palaces erected.

THE OLYMPICS

The goal of the Olympics is to "create a way of life based on . . . the educational value of good example and respect for universal fundamental ethical principles."

—The Olympic Charter[13]

The United Nations was established to help bring peace to a war-torn world. The Olympic Games were established to blend sport with culture and education, bringing people together in peace to respect universal moral principles. Every four years, the Olympic Games are a keenly awaited international spectacle and many would agree that it fosters, however briefly, global goodwill. From a governance perspective, however, the International Olympic Committee (IOC) is a bit of a mess. Members of the IOC are considered public officials under the U.S. anti-bribery law in recognition of the office of public trust that they hold. Marc Hodler was an IOC member for 43 years and finally blew the whistle on long-running abuses. Speaking at IOC headquarters in Lausanne, Switzerland, in 1998, Hodler announced that between 5 and 7 percent of IOC members had solicited bribes for their votes.[14] He claimed that one IOC member had an intermediary, an "agent" working on his behalf to solicit bribes. At the same conference, he announced that bribery had played a role in the selection of Atlanta, Sydney, Nagano and, now famously, Salt Lake City as sites for both summer and winter Olympics. Hodler focused specifically on Salt Lake City's bid for the Winter Olympics, describing the scholarships at local universities that were offered to the children of IOC members, but he added that, to his knowledge, "there has always, always, been a certain part of the vote given to corruption."[15]

After the Salt Lake City scandal in 2002, IOC vice president Un Yong Kim returned to Korea with a "most severe warning" from the IOC for his involvement. There, on June 3, 2004,[16] the Seoul Central District Court found him guilty of stealing millions of dollars from the World Taekwondo Federation that he had led and accepting an additional US$700,000 in bribes.[17] Kim was sentenced to two and a half years imprisonment, later reduced by the Seoul Court of Appeal in September 2004 in recognition of his "service to sport." It wasn't until Kim had exhausted his appeal to the Supreme Court of the Republic of Korea and was actually serving his prison sentence that Kim's colleagues on the IOC met to consider his expulsion from the committee for having "violated the ethical principles set out in the Olympic Charter and the Code of Ethics." He was expelled from the committee on February 4, 2005.

Vancouver will host the next Winter Olympics in 2010. Almost a year before a decision was made about who would host the 2014 Winter Games, proactive government officials were getting a head start on bribery. Sochi is a Black Sea resort town in the Caucasus and it was on the shortlist to host the 2014 Winter Games. In August 2006, Russian police arrested Sergei Evdokimenko, the government official responsible for federal property in Sochi, and charged him with blackmail and soliciting bribes. After a businessman hoping to be awarded Olympic construction contracts was unable to meet Evdokimenko's US$500,000 demand, he cooperated with the Interior Ministry to catch the negotiations on camera.[18] Mr. Evdokimenko was arrested after he was handed the half-million dollar bribe, which presumably would have bought Olympic construction contracts, assuming Sochi was selected.

Once the host city for the Olympics has been selected, the bribery often begins in earnest. Siemens, a German company based in Munich, is one of the world's largest electrical engineering companies. The company aggressively pursued business opportunities available in Athens in the lead up to the Summer Olympics to be held there in 2004 and is alleged to have paid bribes to Greek government officials in an effort to land a major security contract for the Games.[19] Since then, Siemens' difficulties in Athens have been overshadowed by problems closer to home, where six former and current employees were taken into custody in December 2006 as a part of the German government's investigation into 420 million euro (US$540 million) in suspicious payments.[20]

With the Summer Olympics scheduled to take place in Beijing in 2008, the Chinese government has its hands full. According to a spokesman for the Beijing Organizing Committee for the Olympic Games, the government is "paying a lot of attention to [its] anti-corruption work in order to ensure an honest and clean Olympic Games."[21] This comment followed the announcement that Beijing's vice mayor in charge of construction for the Olympics was fired for, among other things, demanding and accepting bribes.[22] According to one report, former Vice Mayor Liu Zhihua's proclivities came to light when a jilted foreign businessman reported him. Apparently, Lui had failed to deliver approval for a land deal after the businessman had paid the bribe demanded. With contracts for the Olympics expected to exceed US$16 billion, managing the risk of bribery during the lead up to the Games is a daunting task.

Once the Summer Games begin, international fellowship and goodwill are meant to take over. That's the theory. In fact, bribery has plagued not only the infrastructure for the Games, but the events themselves. Spectators watching the gold medal boxing match at the 1988 Seoul Olympics saw a fight dominated by American Roy Jones Jr.. When Korean boxer Park Si-hun took gold, an investigation ensued and the judges ultimately conceded that they had been bribed by Korean officials to vote against Jones.[23] Former International Skating Union official, Sally Anne Stapleford, watched the 2006 Turin Winter Olympics from her home in England.[24] Four years earlier in Salt Lake City, it was Stapleford who blew the whistle on Marie-Reine Le Gougne, a French ice-skating judge. Le Gougne had cast the decisive vote at the 2002 Winter Olympics that gave the gold to Russian skaters Yelena Berezhnaya and Anton Sikharulidze and left Canadian favorites, David Pelletier and Jamie Sale, with the silver. Le Gougne later admitted to Stapleford, and then to other IOC officials, that her vote for the Russians was cast in exchange for the Russian vote for a French couple in the ice-dancing competition. When the scandal broke, the IOC president ensured that the Canadians were also awarded gold. Surprisingly, Stapleford has been banned from officiating at the Winter Olympics for her role in exposing the scandal, while Marie-Reine Le Gougne's eligibility has been restored after a three-year ban. Nothing more was said about the role, if any, of the mysterious Russians who struck the deal with Le Gougne.[25]

INTERNATIONAL HUMANITARIAN AID

An estimated 300,000 people were killed on December 26, 2004, when the largest tsunami on record hit the coasts of eleven Asian and

Africa nations. Aid flowed into the region at an unprecedented rate. Governments of the world responded by pledging US$7.1 billion in aid.[26] Nongovernmental organizations sent unprecedented levels of humanitarian aid in the form of money and goods. Where there is aid of that magnitude, there are likely to be government officials hoping to profit, even when the backdrop is one of such utter devastation. The U.S. Agency for International Development was sufficiently concerned about the risk of diversion of funds that a portion of the aid provided was earmarked for a Commission to Investigate Allegations of Bribery and Corruption and for training for civil society to monitor and report on the distribution of tsunami-related aid.[27] The Sri Lankan auditor-general reported that less than half a billion—just 13 percent—of the US$3.2 billion dollars in aid for Sri Lanka's tsunami recovery had been spent.[28] Another article estimates that 30–40 percent of funds sent to Indonesia for tsunami relief were "lost" as a result of corruption.[29] The cost to the international community is considerable when confidence that aid dollars will reach their intended target falters. The pace of donations slows or, in some cases, is reversed. An unnamed German donor withdrew 1 million euro (US$1.3 million) in financial assistance for tsunami victims after reports of corruption in management of the aid.[30] Victims of international disasters, often starkly and immediately vulnerable, suffer first from the disaster, again from the theft or embezzlement of funds designated for their aid, and finally from the cynicism that leads to reduced funding.

THE WORLD BANK: STEALING ON CREDIT

The World Bank's mission statement begins: "To fight poverty with passion and professionalism for lasting results."[31] Unfortunately, before the Bank first began taking bribery seriously, the cost of bribery to borrowing states was two-fold. The loans they accepted increased national debt, as agreed. But the benefit to be derived was partly or wholly undermined by government officials who siphoned off funds for themselves until the purpose of the loan was thwarted. The situation was complicated further by the Bank's position that bribery was a political question and so not within the Bank's purview.

In a report issued in 2004, the Bank described cases in which local politicians were using Bank funds to pay for their political campaigns. The Bank also has reported on investigations into projects for which significant disbursements had been made, but with little progress on the underlying contracts.[32] Two case studies are circulated by Bank staff as a part of presentations on the challenges of bribery in Bank projects. The first involves funding of a road in Haiti. By the time the funds were completely exhausted, nothing had been built but the sign announcing the new, Bank-funded, road. The second includes a photograph of a new school, built with Bank funds. The school was to replace the shaky thatched huts that the children had studied in previously, perched precariously on small stools and balancing their books on their laps. In this case, the school was in fact built, but Bank employees found the new school filled with a local official's onions, drying in the new shelter, and the children still studying nearby in their overcrowded hut.[33]

The United Nations, international aid organizations, the Olympics— even the World Bank with its express goal of poverty alleviation—can cut across national borders to give people hope and a sense of camaraderie and shared purpose. When governance within these organizations fails, however, when they are brought low by bribery scandals and rampant abuses of official office, the cynicism is commensurately grave. If these well-funded organizations with their lofty mission statements and laudable goals are riddled with bribery, how much more difficult will it be for remote communities far from the media to root out bribery and ensure transparency?

Chapter 7

Preying on the Public

People have no idea how directly proportional the existence of corruption is to the misery of our people.

—Luis Roberto Mesquita, Brazilian businessman and anti-bribery activist, acceptance speech for Integrity Award, 2002

BRIBERY FROM BIRTH

The misery caused by commercial bribery is real, but indirect. The direct and immediate suffering caused by other forms of bribery is as nearly impossible to measure as it is to overstate. Over time, government officials, broadly defined to include politicians, civil servants, and employees of state-run institutions, have turned every imaginable task into a revenue source. Greed has known no bounds and dignity has been shown no quarter. This chapter is about the darkest, most offensive corners of extortionate activity.

The first few days of motherhood can be a frightening time under ideal circumstances.[1] The newness of the role, the apparent fragility of the baby, and the almost overwhelming machinery of the medical community designed to quickly deliver, assess, and discharge the new baby combine to challenge the confidence of a new mother. This is true under ideal circumstances. Imagine this scene instead.[2] A new mother delivers her baby and—before she has touched it, before she has even seen it—it is removed from the delivery room. The nurse returns without the baby to demand a payment. At a time when a young mother's instincts are focused on ensuring the safety of her new baby, she must first negotiate a payment that won't bankrupt her family. The going rate for the first glimpse of your baby in Bangalore is US$12 for a baby boy. The rate for a baby girl is just US$7. Presumably, new parents have to take the nurse's word with respect to the gender of a baby they haven't seen yet. In an excellent article on this practice, reporter Celia Dugger of the *New York Times* interviewed a new grandmother who had braced herself for the anticipated extortion: "she was determined to pay no more than US$7."[3] She was able to hold her ground. Her monthly wages were just US$10.

In some countries the havoc wrought by bribery comes a bit later in childhood. China is trying to crack down on child trafficking, a problem reluctantly acknowledged by the government.[4] Babies and young children are stolen from hospitals and homes and transported to rural China or overseas. In Guangxi province in July 2006, 28 babies were intercepted on a bus, "drugged and bound in nylon duffel bags."[5] Fifty-two ring members were convicted. Gangs are well-organized and trafficking is profitable because of the difficulty of adopting legally through China's formal adoption system. It is simpler to buy a baby from the traffickers. Afterwards, one need only bribe the appropriate government officials to "legalize" the adoption.[6] The reported willingness of some Chinese officials to facilitate the theft of children by providing the false paperwork has frustrated efforts to stop the practice.

BRIBERY AND EDUCATION

In rigid educational systems like some in Asia, exams begin in early childhood and narrow the pool of students who can reach the best high schools and, from there, the top universities. The pressure on students is considerable and, in some schools, ability takes a distant second place to cash when it's time for grades. A computer data professor in Ho Chi Minh City Open University ended up in prison after accepting US$685 in bribes in exchange for helping eleven students pass exams.[7] An administrator and teacher in China didn't even require their students to make a gesture toward passing their exams and conspired instead to change the scores of ninety-seven students in 2005 after the fact. They pocketed over a million yuan (US$128,000) in the process.[8] Many teachers are not introduced to bribery for the first time when they reach the classroom. A journalist in Cambodia reported on a scandal there in late 2006. Teachers, it turned out, were required to pay bribes of between US$300 and US$450 to education officials in order to secure permanent, government teaching positions.[9]

This educational system is rigged from the outset if bribe-payers secure the jobs, and students willing to pay bribes advance through the system. It is reasonable to conclude that students who advance to top universities and excel once there, at least occasionally through bribery, are likely to rise to positions of power—positions from which they can, if they choose, extort bribes from another generation of aspiring bureaucrats.

BRIBERY AND LIVELIHOOD

Bribery interferes with the ability of millions to earn a reasonable living. Taxi drivers seem particularly vulnerable and face demands for bribes in exchange for licenses from Czechoslovakia[10] to Afghanistan, where the head of a regional traffic department hit one taxi company up for US$12,000.[11] Restaurant owners are expected to pay bribes to satisfy health inspectors[12] and building inspectors.[13] A prominent Brazilian politician resigned his legislative seat to face allegations of demanding bribes from the owner of a restaurant.[14] Once prosperous cocoa farmers working in the Ivory Coast get just twenty-five cents per pound for their crop now, but must pay the truck drivers US$2,000 to deliver their crops to market. The first thousand covers the drivers' costs; the second thousand covers the bribes for soldiers who extort payments along the way.[15]

BRIBERY AND LOSS OF LIBERTY

For a shadowy international community, an exchange of bribes results in the loss of liberty and a life spent in often unspeakable conditions. These people—typically, but not exclusively women—are often lured with job offers and then sold, defrauded, or coerced into labor against their will. They may be compelled to work in the agricultural sector, domestic service or the international sex trade. Their identity documents are typically confiscated and they are confined to their owners' property, and usually prevented from learning the local language to further increase their isolation.

According to Interpol, "[t]rafficking in women for sexual exploitation is a multi-billion-dollar business which involves citizens of most countries and helps sustain organized crime."[16] The whole sordid industry is viable only when bribery flourishes. Local police officers accept "bribes or free sexual services in exchange for protecting—or just overlooking the illegality of—of brothels."[17] Police also accept bribes to tip-off brothel owners if a raid is imminent so that they can "secure" the trafficked women and especially those who are underage.[18] If girls or women are detained by the police, brothel owners may, in some cases, be able to buy them back from corrupt authorities.[19] In one reported incident, a trafficking victim described local policemen driving minor girls who had escaped back to the brothel. In this account, the return of the girls was followed by gunshots and the removal of two small bodies, wrapped in carpets.[20] Low-level government officials accept bribes in exchange for normalizing immigration documents or for looking the other way when passports are clearly fake.[21]

"Official complicity is almost required for the trafficking and enslavement of human beings to occur. The malfeasance of local officials undermines local authorities of integrity and purpose, and erodes the achievements that their countrymen and women have secured at high cost."[22] Bribes buy that complicity.

BRIBERY AND DEATH

Even the dead are not beyond the reach of bribery. When the mother of Himanshu Sharma learned of his suicide, she travelled to the mortuary of the All-India Institute of Medical Sciences to retrieve his body.[23] The inspector there demanded a payment of 11,000 Rupees (US$248) to certify that suicide was the cause of death and to release the body to his family. After the inspector reportedly threatened to record the death as murder, the family paid him, afraid that he would frame them in a fabricated murder case. The inspector then demanded an additional 15,000 Rupees (US$338) to pay off other officials.[24] With the cooperation of the family, the second transaction was caught on film and the inspector suspended. In China, where government-run morgues can't handle the volume, employees are alleged to have accepted bribes from family members to ensure the bodies of their relatives are stored properly and not "piled up" or "placed on the floor."[25]

COUNTERFEIT DRUGS

Chapter 5 describes the problem of pharmaceutical companies that make payments to doctors in exchange for prescribing their medicine. There is another transactional layer below this, however, and one that is more worrying. A senior executive with a U.S. pharmaceutical company recounted a story of bribery in West Africa.[26] The company produces a medicine that enhances the immunity of those suffering from debilitating diseases. In this case, however, thugs importing a counterfeit product, marked with the company's name, were able to break into the market and get their fake product in circulation. They did this, it is assumed, by paying off customs officials and, quite possibly, the local health authorities. The chain reaction of misery that this set off was startling. First, of course, was the damage to the health of the patients who relied on the medicine which was inert in some cases and actively dangerous in others. Consumed as they were by people with compromised immune systems, the results were described as devastating. While the human suffering was more serious than anything that followed, the rest should not be overlooked. The reputation of the pharmaceutical company suffered terribly in the local community. The counterfeit drugs had been marked with the company's name. Ultimately, the company was required to defend against legal action for the injury inflicted by the drugs which they hadn't made, sanctioned, or profited from. The interests of the two parties that had important, urgent and legitimate business to transact—the pharmaceutical company and the patient—were shoved aside by the criminals who manufactured the dangerous alternative and the string of government officials that were paid not to inspect, paid not to test, and so paid not to keep their citizens safe.

EXTORTIONATE UN AID WORKERS AND PEACEKEEPING FORCES

There are ways to abuse power for private gain that do not involve an exchange of cash or goods. Liberia, accrediting government of the diploma mill described previously, struggles to recover from a fourteen-year civil war that ended in 2003. Thousands of children have been orphaned by the conflict. The country's infrastructure has been destroyed. An uneasy peace is maintained by the United Nations peacekeeping troops and international aid is coordinated and delivered by, among others, the UN World Food Programme (WFP). The WFP has set "the well-oiled wheels of its emergency response procedure into motion. Over its forty year history, the agency has turned the complex business of getting the right food to the right people in the right place into a fine science."[27] Part of the WFP strategy is to build temporary communities in which refugees from the civil war can gather safely and begin to rebuild their communities. Schools are often established for the children. "WFP kick-starts development by paying workers with rations to build vital infrastructure and offering children food aid as a reward for going to school."[28] The problems begin when the UN WFP employees—public officials carrying diplomatic UN passports and entitled to the privileged and immunities afforded that organization—begin to put their own interest ahead of their official responsibilities. In a region in which a successful refugee can earn, with effort, just under a dollar per day, opportunities for significant self-enrichment are remote. These officials have, however, found a way to turn their positions of authority to their own advantage.

Findings based on 315 interviews by Save the Children indicated that some WFP employees required young girls, including girls under fourteen years of age, to exchange sex for their rations and school fees.[29] Although children interviewed said that UN vehicles are occasionally used, the grim exchange often takes place right in the camp housing: "[sexual exploitation] was more in the camp as some children had their own shelters and it was very common to have sex."[30] Parents described being unable to watch over their children: "All children are at risk in the camps because of the hard living conditions, the lack of money, children and parents not sleeping in the same place. . . Parents have to go out and look for cash and children are left on their own."[31]

In a June 2006 brochure, "HIV/AIDS & Children: Bringing Hope to a Generation," the WFP highlights the problem of children earning money by any means available. "This can mean being forced into activities such as survival sex—the trading of sex for food and money—that put them at even greater risk of contracting HIV.[32] Children who trade sex, what they call "man business," for rations to which they are entitled as a part of the mandate of both WFP and its donors—WFP is funded entirely by voluntary contributions—risk pregnancy, social stigma, and disease.

Another category of UN officials engaged in extortion of this kind is the peacekeepers based in Liberia. While it is certainly not the case that all or even a majority of UN officials are engaged in this practice, the Save the Children report did recount that "sexual exploitation of children by peacekeeping soldiers was described in every location where a contingent was stationed."[33] This is disturbing not only for the obvious reasons, but also because the UN has repeatedly stressed that the credibility and success of UN peacekeeping forces, which are or have been at the heart of international crises in Lebanon, East Timor, Sudan, and Kosovo, depend on the ability of the troops to establish relationships based on trust in the local communities.[34]

These allegations are not disputed by the United Nations.[35] The protocol, according to UN regulations, is for victims of this sort of extortion to be encouraged to report wrongdoers. The Save the Children report indicated, however, that the Camp Management Committee and block leaders within the camp were also involved in the exchanges. As such, members of what must be among the most vulnerable communities in the world—undernourished, homeless, battered by a war as old as many of them—were encouraged by the UN to report the activity to those who controlled their housing, distributed their food and were themselves active in the abuses of power.

WHISTLEBLOWERS

Reaching out to those who would disclose abuses by government officials presents a unique set of challenges. Those vulnerable to such abuses are already at a disadvantage and are likely to fear retaliation from those in power and keen to hold on to it. They may not have access to secure communications channels and, in the rare cases in which they do, they may not know who to contact and whether they can trust them. The other side of this is protection of those about whom reports are made. Basic principles of due process require that allegations not be aired as fact when the professional standing and reputation of those involved are at risk. Nevertheless, in the world of bribery and extortion, the odds are typically stacked against the person of whom the demand is made, the person who starts with little and stands to lose even that or the person who makes a moral choice to expose a scheme.

   In the latter category, those who make the difficult choice to expose
a bribery scheme, many must be recognized for their decision posthu-
mously. Satyendra Dubey was a thirty-one year old senior engineer and
graduate of the prestigious Indian Institute of Technology working on
one of the largest infrastructure projects in India: the Golden Quadri-
lateral Highway, part of a US$12 billion highway project. According to
Dubey, the project to build over 8,000 miles of highway was riddled
with bribery and he, like many young professional Indians, was tired of
it.[36] He sat down and wrote a long letter to Prime Minister Atal Behari
Vajpayee describing the looting of public money, hijacked procurement
process, and mismanagement, which was delivered on November 11,
2003. The project was vast, however, and he was concerned that his
letter would be dismissed without proper consideration. In an effort
to ensure that his letter was taken seriously, he attached a cover letter describing his position and his first-hand experience of the culture
of bribery surrounding the project. Appearing nervous, he then asked
that the cover letter be detached before the underlying allegations were
forwarded for investigation "to ensure secrecy."[37] The cover letter was
not detached and Dubey's name was circulated widely. After complain-
ing of death threats for several months, Dubey was shot to death. No
one has been found guilty of the crime, but it has been the government's position that his murder was the result of a routine robbery.
One suspect escaped while being taken into custody and, of the three
witnesses, one has disappeared and the other two are alleged to have
committed suicide, both by poison, a day apart.[38]

Chapter 8

Mounting Impatience

We know what corruption has cost us—it has denied us the value of our resources, both human and natural. It breeds injustice. It causes killings, the diseases that ravage us almost everywhere. It turns us into a country of people who live on the kindness of others and we are very angry. This is not what we want, and this is not what we are going to allow to continue.

—Nuhu Ribadu, Chairman of the Nigerian Economic and Financial Crimes Commission, World Bank Annual Meeting, Singapore, September 17, 2006[1]

ONE SMALL COUNTRY LEADS THE WAY

Mr. Ribadu is speaking of the miseries that bribery and corruption have brought in Nigeria. Clearly he is impatient and understands the dimensions of the damage bribery has done in his country. For a still clearer manifestation of impatience and frustration, it is instructive to look at the experience of Lesotho with the World Bank-financed project that was expected to lift that country out of severe poverty. Instead, the Highwaters dams project has meant expensive and ultimately disappointing prosecutions by a state that insisted that the law be respected.[2]

Bribery, we are told, is primarily a problem in developing countries, where wages are low, oversight is weak, dictators prevail, and government as a whole is broken. Companies bribe with impunity in many instances. No one is doing anything to curb demand-side bribery. The pessimists who utter such statements might have predicted that the people of Lesotho would remain silent, or perhaps even encourage, acts of bribery on their soil. But people in some countries have had enough. Lesotho showed the international community that countries are increasingly willing to speak out against the toll that bribery takes on their communities. Some are prepared to act against their short term financial interests and to bear the administrative and financial cost of a long and hard-fought legal process to root out and punish parties to bribery.

In 1998, the waters had been rising for three years behind the Katse Dam. As they approached the crest of the dam, the floodgates were opened and water started flowing down through eighty miles of pipes and tunnels, out of the mountains of the small kingdom of Lesotho down to the broad plains of the rich and industrialized Gauteng province of South Africa. The newly constructed dam enabled Lesotho, a country with no gold or diamonds—with next to no industry of any kind—to harvest its only marketable natural resource, water, and to deliver it to South Africa in return for about US$20 million per year.

More than 80 percent of Lesotho's land is over a mile above sea level; less than a tenth can support crops. Lesotho is engulfed by South Africa physically and financially. South Africa supports King Letsie III of Lesotho. Former South African president Nelson Mandela attended his coronation; current president Thabo Mbeki was fined one large cow by the new king for his failure to attend.

The traditional fines and ceremonies are appealing, but the degree of dependence is not. Forty percent of Lesotho wage earners labor in South Africa, most of them in its mines.[3] Forty-nine percent of its population lives below the poverty line and 30 percent are HIV positive.[4] The average life expectancy for Basotho, citizens of Lesotho, is under 35 years. Lesotho is the sort of miserably impoverished, undemocratic state that wealthy developed countries point to when they argue that commercial bribery is unavoidable because of the nature of the markets in which their multinational companies must operate. The US$8 billion Lesotho dam project was exactly the sort of massive infrastructure project that anti-bribery experts describe as rife with opportunity for all manner of bribery and extortion.

The Katse Dam, which was the centerpiece of the first of a five-phase construction project to bring the waters of the Lesotho highlands down to South Africa's plains, at once became a source of immense pride for the Basotho people. Feasibility studies were completed in 1978 and the Lesotho Highlands Water Authority was created in 1986. In November of that year, Mr. Musapha Ephraim Sole, a Lesotho-born, Canadian-educated civil engineer with fourteen years of service in the Department of Water Affairs, was appointed the first director of the authority. He began reviewing bids from many of the world's major construction companies for the US$2 billion first phase of the US$8 billion project.

The water projects at once dwarfed all other aspects of the Lesotho economy. Reports written in the mid-1990s predicted that within twenty-five years six dams and a huge hydroelectric generating plant would be built. These public works, unprecedented in the history of the mountain kingdom, were expected to bring with them modernity, wealth, scores of thousands of jobs, and even tourism.

Dams generally bring a good deal of resistance as well, particularly from international environmental groups and even from the World Bank itself,[5] but also from the local people downstream who will lose their water and the people upstream who will lose their land. In Lesotho, however, there was little protest, even during "resettlement" of local communities. The project brought hope to the people of Lesotho and, on the whole, the people supported it.

The first two dams, Katse and Mahole, were completed in the mid-1990s. By late 1998, work related to the project amounted to 13.6 percent of Lesotho's entire gross domestic product.[6] As early as 1991, however, rumors surrounded project director Musapha Sole who was living very large on his modest government official's salary.

In the early 1990s, Sole, director of the Lesotho Highwaters Development Project (LHDP), faced a routine audit by Ernst & Young. After the audit uncovered irregularities in Sole's accounts, disciplinary hearings were held; Sole was suspended in October 1994 and then dismissed in November 1995.[7]

Sole was then sued in civil court by the LHDP for damages they alleged he caused the project, and during the course of pre-trial discovery, bank records came to light revealing his half dozen secret bank accounts in Zurich and Geneva. The accounts contained the equivalent of over two million dollars in British pounds, French francs, German marks and Canadian dollars. Government officials in Lesotho did not ask Sole for a cut as many might have expected under the circumstances. Instead, they initiated criminal charges against Sole.[8]

From the outset, prosecuting authorities, under the direction of Mr. Fine Maema, Attorney General of Lesotho, experienced tremendous difficulties. Without evidence of an underlying crime, the Swiss authorities declined to release information about transfers into and out of the accounts in Zurich and Geneva. World Bank officials argued that the matter should be settled swiftly and quietly lest the entire Highwaters project be imperiled. The various contractors involved in the engineering and construction exerted pressure through their home governments to have Sole quickly replaced so the project could move forward.

On May 20, 1999, Attorney General Maema won a court victory in Geneva that led to better cooperation from the Swiss authorities. Switzerland's highest court decided to extend legal assistance to Lesotho's investigation—a judgment in line with other legal developments as Switzerland adopted and implemented the anti-bribery principles of the Organization for Economic Cooperation and Development.[9] From June onward, Maema enjoyed strong support from the Swiss Office for Police Matters, and very rapidly an illuminating "paper trail" emerged. It supported most of the suspicions surrounding Sole. By the second half of 1999, the Attorney General made it clear that he had both a compelling circumstantial case against Sole and a resolute determination to prosecute him for bribery, fraud, and perjury.

When this hard documentary evidence emerged, the attitude of the World Bank finally shifted. On November 17, 1999, the World Bank hosted a meeting in Pretoria, South Africa to discuss the impending prosecution of Sole. Attorney General Maema explained:

> This meeting was called by the World Bank and was attended by repre-
> sentatives of various role players concerned with the Highlands Water
> Project, including representatives from South Africa, Britain, the Euro-
> pean Union, the European Investment bank, individual banks in Europe,
> and so on. At this meeting the actions of the Lesotho government were
> praised. More importantly, from various quarters, promises were made of
> assistance in these prosecutions. This was after the representatives from
> Lesotho had pointed out to those present that these prosecutions would
> constitute a considerable drain on Lesotho's financial resources.[10]

Two months before that meeting and weeks after Attorney General Maema first made it clear that he was determined to prosecute Sole, the World Bank vice presidents for the Africa region, Callisto E. Madavo and Jen-Louis Sarbib, expressed support for Lesotho's efforts to investigate and end bribery associated with the dam project. "We are proud—that the World Bank played a leading role in making this important project happen, even if our financial contribution was less than 5 percent of total costs. Our commitment to preventing corruption extends well beyond our financial involvement in a project. Corruption hurts the poor most of all—whether it involves aid, private investment or the use of a developing country's own taxpayers' money. We are determined to help African countries fight corruption in all its forms."[11]

Only a few days after the Pretoria meeting, on December 3, 1999, Attorney General Maema released his indictment of Sole. The shock for the other parties who attended the Pretoria meeting was that he released eighteen other indictments at the same time, including indictments against most of the major multinational corporations who had received large contracts to work on the dam project.[12] This was clearly unexpected, especially by the participants in the Pretoria meeting. Their surprise was compounded when Lesotho's home affairs minister, Motsoahae Thabane, declared repeatedly, "It takes two to tango. . . . We want to prove that big companies cannot come here, walk around and bribe people. We know that the case hasn't gone down well with the mother countries of the companies involved, which is strange because they are the preachers of the highest standards of morality, and we are following their script."[13]

The various companies energetically protested their innocence in the strongest terms. Oskar Sigvaldson, president of Canadian firm Acres International stated: "We are not guilty and we are confident that we will be cleared of all allegations." Peter Brettell, managing director of Sir Alexander Gibb & Partners of the United Kingdom: "We will be vigorously defending our position and we deny all the charges."

A spokesman in Milan for Impregilo: "We are absolutely confident the judge will clear us of any wrong-doing."[14]

Spokesmen for various companies declared that they had been unaware that the payments they were making to their commercial agents in Lesotho, which in some cases amounted to 5 percent of the total cost of the contract, were being passed through to Sole. When their position became less plausible as the agents were prosecuted and confessed their roles, the companies maintained instead that although they had made the payments, they had been the victims of extortion.

These cases were hard-fought at every turn. The defendants were able to convince the court that "consortia as such, as opposed to their individual members, could not be held criminally responsible. . . [and that] the court [should] order a separation of trials. With this result the prosecuting authorities [were compelled to deal] with each role player in this whole saga separately."[15] These rulings meant that the prosecutions would be far costlier and far slower. The Attorney General was forced to withdraw his initial December 1999 multiple indictment and submit new and separate indictments in June 2001.

Sole was the first to stand trial, with Acres International to follow. As Sole's trial commenced in June 2001, the World Bank project director for the Lesotho Highwaters project, Mr. Andrew Macoun, announced that the Bank had carried out its own investigation of Acres International through its Investigations Panel and found it had insufficient evidence for any action against Acres.

Macoun spoke out again in December 2001 to announce that the World Bank would not, in fact, fund Lesotho's prosecution costs. In a short statement without explanation, Macoun "confirmed the World Bank would not be contributing to Lesotho's legal costs." He added that "successful prosecution of the companies would result in fines that would recoup the government's legal costs." In subsequent weeks the European Union, Britain, and others also withdrew their promises of support, or simply failed to deliver on them.[16] A few months later, in February 2002, the World Bank declared it would not debar any of the fourteen western multinational corporations accused in the Lesotho case. To date, the government of Lesotho also has received very little encouragement from international organizations entrusted with the task of combating bribery.

An Irish-born judge, Justice Brendan Cullinan, formerly the chief justice of the Lesotho High Court, was called out of retirement to try the cases. About the time his bench trial began, Sole was involved in a minor car accident and subsequently appeared in court prone, in a hospital bed. (During the course of the trial he also ran for parliament and won a seat in the opposition, though his subsequent conviction prevented his taking the seat.) Sole was silent throughout the trial, refusing to testify in his own defense and calling no witnesses.[17]

Justice Cullinan found that Sole had been involved in forty-eight corrupt or fraudulent transactions over a period of nine years, and that he had accepted bribes from twelve contractors. Cullinan imposed eleven sentences to serve concurrently resulting in eighteen years in prison. Sole was also required to disgorge more than a million dollars in improper payments received. The conviction was upheld on appeal though the sentence was shortened by three years. Sole's property was attached and his bank accounts frozen; he relied on legal aid for his appeal.

On September 17, 2002, the High Court in Lesotho handed down its second conviction in the bribery trials: Acres International, the Canadian construction consulting firm, was found guilty of paying US$266,000 in bribes to Sole. Speaking in October 2002, World Bank spokesperson Caroline Anstey declared, "We said at the time [that is, in February when the Bank announced it would not be debarring any of the multinationals involved in the Lesotho projects] that if the prosecution in Lesotho—which is a criminal prosecution with subpoena power (which we don't have)—came up with new evidence involving any other companies we looked at, we would be prepared to reopen the investigation."[18] The record of transactions in Swiss banks would have been new evidence to the World Bank Sanctions Committee, as would later guilty pleas by two persons who served as couriers for payments to Sole, but the Bank initially affirmed its ruling that there was insufficient evidence to debar any of the large multinationals. It pointed out that it did, however, debar two companies implicated in the case. Both were Panama-based front companies used to launder bribes on their way to Sole. But because Panama's opaque corporate laws permit secret ownership of companies, within twenty-four hours, replacement companies could have been established to replace the two debarred by the Bank.[19]

On November 3, 2002, Acres International was sentenced to pay a fine of US$2.25 million. Five weeks later Acres was able to secure a suspension of payment of the fine pending the outcome of an appeal. By that time, the various trials had cost between four and five million dollars. Lesotho had to bear the costs of these expensive trials and appeals while defendants and their legal teams found new delaying tactics.

Leaba Thetsane, director of public prosecutions in Lesotho, has declared that Lesotho will "continue relentlessly" in trying the bribery allegations. "The Acres fine doesn't cover the enormous bills we've run up investigating and prosecuting these cases, but it helps. . . . We've had real financial difficulties but we're determined to fight corruption and have had government's support all the way."

Acres lost its final appeal in 2003. On July 23, 2004, Acres was declared ineligible to receive any new Bank financed contracts for a three-year period.

Also in 2003, the Lesotho High Court handed down a second corporate conviction, this time to the German engineering firm Lahmeyer International which was sentenced to pay a criminal fine of US$1.46 million. On November 6, 2006, the Bank declared Laymeyer ineligible to receive any new bank financed contracts for a seven-year period.[20]

In February 2004, Schneider Electric of France, which acquired Spie Batignolles, pleaded guilty to sixteen counts of bribery related to the dam project.[21,22] Later in 2004, "a consortium that includes local companies Concor and Group Five, and British and German firms, was convicted for bribery amounting to US$375,000 in the project."[23]

South Africa stepped forward in early 2004 to discuss how the ongoing prosecutions could be funded. According to one report, "Aware of the liabilities facing Lesotho, such as costly appeals from companies found guilty of corruption and new prosecutions against companies and local officials, Water Affairs and Forestry Minister Ronnie Kasrils held a meeting with his counterpart in Lesotho to discuss ways in which SA could assist."[24]

With a small legal community in Lesotho—judges were called out of retirement and prosecutors were called in from South Africa—and with few financial resources, Lesotho secured convictions, repeatedly upheld on appeal, while the World Bank and the countries in which the companies were headquartered did little. It was not until after it was clear that Lesotho would not relent that others acted.[25] Lesotho provides a powerful response to those who believe that commercial transactions in Africa are irredeemably riddled with bribery and to those who believe no government in the region will stand against it.

It is still not clear why Lesotho took the stand that it did, when it did. Cynics could argue that Sole had failed to buy broad enough support for his scheme. He appears to have acted almost alone. More likely, the tiny kingdom had so little experience with commerce on this scale that they hadn't had time to grow cynical and nationalism and pride carried the day. In any event, Attorney General Maema has stated that "Lesotho is committed to completing these prosecutions, primarily in order to eradicate corruption in Lesotho, but also to set an example for other countries. . . . Other countries will realize that corruption can be combated successfully, provided the necessary will is there and also that the countries involved give each other the necessary support."[26]

Construction on the first phase of the Lesotho Highwaters project is complete. South Africa revised downward its projected need for water from Lesotho and has placed on hold subsequent phases. The people of Lesotho have probably seen the end of this massive project.

The actions of the companies involved in this bribery scandal were not especially egregious. They paid commercial intermediaries while either knowing or not bothering to ask where the money would end up. Companies operating in Africa have done far worse. They probably assumed that the payments to Sole would be lost in the vast project and that, if they were noticed at all, it would be deemed "business as usual" for another African country. Lesotho surprised them. By pursuing even one allegation of bribery on even one government contract, a country can create a powerful deterrent. Those who pay bribes, and those who take them, count on those nearby either not to notice or not to care. By introducing any cost to the transaction at all, there is the chance that one party will be too fearful to discuss a bribery scheme. Bribery thrives in darkened corners and wilts under bright lights. The trials, expense, and distraction continue, but Lesotho has earned for itself a reputation that countries with experienced and well-financed enforcement agencies must envy.

While unique in its tenacity in pursuing both bribe-payers and bribe-recipient, Lesotho reflects an international trend of increasing impatience with commercial bribery. Norms change slowly and this is particularly so when those in power profit from the status quo and control the machinery that might bring change: new laws, the media, investigative and enforcement agencies, and the judiciary. This can mean that countries with the highest levels of bribery are slowest to change. Over the last few years, however, countries traditionally thought to suffer from high levels of bribery have shown a surprising willingness to adopt aggressive new anti-bribery laws.

Thirty years ago, the United States was the first country to enact a law that criminalized bribery of foreign officials. It wasn't until the mid-1990s that international conventions against bribery really caught on, but the world quickly had more conventions than it strictly needed to do the job.[27] In 1996, the Organization of American States was the first group to adopt a convention criminalizing international bribery. The Inter-American Convention Against Corruption, ratified by 33 of its 34 member countries,[28] was an ambitious law. Unlike the FCPA, which addresses only supply-side bribery, this Convention made it a crime both for individuals and companies to give and for government officials to receive bribes. It looked good on paper, but ten years later several countries still haven't adopted laws that draw the international instrument down into their domestic laws. With no enforcement mechanism, this Convention remains an elegant, but largely ineffective, grand statement of principle.

Shortly thereafter, in 1997, the Organization for Economic Cooperation and Development (OECD) adopted its Convention on Combating Bribery of Foreign Public Officials in International Business Transactions. The OECD is an organization of thirty of the world's wealthiest nations, including most of Europe, North America, and, in the Pacific Rim, Australia, New Zealand, Japan, and Korea. With the arrival of the OECD Convention, the United States and a handful of other countries found themselves to be signatories of two such international conventions.

In November 1998, the Council of Europe adopted a Criminal Law Convention on Corruption, largely duplicating the impact of the OECD Convention for most European countries, but expanding the scope of the latter by criminalizing "private-to-private" bribery—the payment of bribes by one private individual or company to another, without the involvement of a government official.[29] It also criminalized "trading in influence," a term that no one fully understands, but that makes lobbyists nervous.

Four years later, in July 2003, the African Union adopted its Convention on Preventing and Combating Corruption. And, finally, the United Nations adopted the first truly international convention in October 2003 with the unfortunate acronym UNCAC: the United Nations Convention Against Corruption. The UNCAC drafters were the beneficiaries of the drafting lessons from the many conventions that had come before and, with 192 UN members, the UNCAC has the broadest reach of any of the anti-bribery conventions. It is difficult to keep these conventions straight, and it is worrying to companies that operate internationally that the provisions of each convention are slightly different. So, what has this 'rush to ratify' done to advance transparency and to reduce the pace and impact of international bribery and extortion? It has enabled the international community, over many high-level summits and then lower-level negotiations, to reflect its constituents' mounting impatience with business as usual.

Conclusion

Modest Optimism

This book has painted a daunting image of the scope and prevalence of bribery. It may have made it appear that the practice of bribing and seeking bribes is flourishing, and it probably is. But the survey of this landscape would be incomplete without an observation of the many indications that bribery can be limited or suppressed and, in some areas, eradicated.

EVOLVING NORMS

Bribery is unlikely ever to be exterminated altogether. We can't simply declare "the moral equivalent of war" on bribery and it won't work to have everyone simply join hands and promise to try harder. It will take a more sensible approach to achieve practical results, but with enough pragmatism and sufficient intelligent attention to the interests of all involved, the noxious practice of bribery may well be successfully suppressed in most places. This chapter will outline some of the ways that can happen, because it is equally foolish to declare that nothing can be done to limit bribery.

It may seem sophisticated or worldly to say that bribery is a product of human nature and that human nature cannot be changed, or that bribery comes of greed and greed will never be satisfied. What may seem sophisticated and worldly is, in this case, merely blasé. It is the path of least resistance to declare that the status quo is immutable, and that path is wrong.

In fact, the norms that guide the behavior of societies with regard to moral issues like slavery, capital punishment or bribery change markedly over time. Ethan Nadelmann has explored and charted the ways norms evolve with an abundance of evidence that leaves little doubt that real and lasting reform is possible.[1] On the anti-bribery front, real progress is underway.

In any case, it should be obvious that the common wisdom doesn't pass the common sense test. Many societies, many cities, many governments, and many corporations have been far more tainted by the practice of bribery at various times in the past than they are today. Bribery was much more common in America during the Grant administration, as evidenced by the Crédit Mobilier affair,[2] than it is today. Bribery was far more out of control in the Harding administration at the time of the Teapot Dome scandal than it is in this century, and neither the Grant nor the Harding administration approached the depths of malfeasance of Boss Tweed and Tammany Hall in New York. If bribery cannot be suppressed, how can it be that these dark, low water marks are a thing of the past?

It might be useful to put bribery in the context of other global patterns of behavior that once were accepted as immutable, but later were isolated, condemned, outlawed, and largely eliminated. Consider piracy and the slave trade. These practices have not been eradicated altogether, but they have been delegitimized in the sense that practices that were once considered the proper business of states now are understood as nothing better than crimes against humanity. Though bribery is unlikely ever to be deemed a crime against humanity, it is well on the way to being delegitimized and cast out.

To pursue the analogy to piracy, two centuries ago, many states at war sheltered pirates. They gave them safe harbors to work from, became their sponsors, offered them the protective coloration of a flag, and lent them legitimacy by issuing them commissions. The elegantly named "letters of marque" were no more than permits to prey on the enemy's shipping and take one's pay out of the spoils. The British themselves, in the days of Elizabeth I, had commissioned Francis Drake to prey on the Spanish. By the 1700s, the British, with their dominant Royal Navy, took a dim view of the practice, but to the Americans in both the War for Independence and the War of 1812, privateering was an indispensable weapon of the weak.

There are pockets of piracy today, but the days of state-sponsored piracy are over. The beginning of the end for state-sponsored piracy came late in the seventeenth century when increased trade between the powers of Europe made stable, cooperative relationships more remunerative than predatory ones. There was more to be gained from dependable, peaceful exchange than from furtive war at sea. Governments growing in strength wanted monopolies on force, so the brigands had to go. Piracy as a national industry receded as piracy as an isolated international threat advanced.

What changed was that those in power recognized a new alignment of their interests. The sentiment that gave rise to piracy—rapacious greed—did not vanish. Rather, the principal actors realized they could prosper better in a more ordered, more regulated system.[3] Governments became champions of law enforcement and piracy, once useful when thinly disguised, was rejected and suppressed.

There is a similar parallel to the slave trade. Britain, France, and other states once depended on and energetically participated in the practice of buying and selling human beings, finding it both profitable and indispensable to the production of sugar in their Caribbean colonies. The British king, his Parliament, and the Anglican Church long avoided any expression of misgivings about a trade that had made Liverpool one of the richest ports in the world.

Their blindness to the brutal wrongness of their own behavior is breathtaking. In 1760, the Archbishop of Canterbury mused on the subject of the welfare of his slaves. His church owned a rich sugar plantation in Barbados called Codrington, and Codrington slaves had the word SOCIETY branded on their chests because they belonged to the missionary wing of the Church, the Society for the Propagation of the Gospel in Foreign Parts. What troubled the archbishop was that the plantation continually had to buy new slaves, around thirty each year. This was because they were losing that many every year to malnutrition, overwork, and disease. He knew what was happening and managed to feel, at least in passing, some concern, but he didn't let it detain him long. "I have long wondered and lamented," he wrote to another bishop, "that the Negroes in our plantations decrease, and new Supplies become necessary continually. Surely this proceeds from some defect, both of humanity, and even of good policy. But we must take things as they are at present."[4]

It wasn't until the interests of the King, the Church, and Parliament changed as England entered the industrial age and exports of manufactured goods produced by wage earners outweighed the agricultural goods produced by slaves that the inequity of slavery became "unbearable." Only at that point did the principles of the Enlightenment finally make it impossible to overlook the gross inhumanity of the slave trade.

International standards do change, and so do laws and practices. What seemed to the archbishop impossible to change in 1760 actually had been outlawed throughout the empire by 1807. By 1833, slavery had been abolished throughout Britain's possessions and almost a quarter of the Royal Navy's ships were employed in the *suppression* of the slave trade. The same slow process of change is at work with bribery.

FEWER PLACES TO HIDE

In recent decades, bribery has lost much of its aura of acceptability as those involved recognized a new alignment of their own interests. Governments of trading nations and corporations with competitive products have found that they don't prosper optimally in a system where contracts are bought and sold to inefficient producers. Where once individual office holders could confidently expect to profit personally by covertly selling their influence to bribe-paying companies, their operations are increasingly exposed for the damaging, costly perversions of good business that they are. The cost to all the participants in the deal is being recognized and the benefit to the corrupt individual is less frequently tolerated.

In a single generation, the world has gone from widespread tolerance to specific intolerance of the practices of corruption. The spate of international conventions discussed in Chapter 8 have created new mechanisms for international cooperation that increase the risk associated with bribery and also make it more difficult for individuals, companies, and government officials to keep the proceeds of bribery. Under the UNCAC in particular, countries have agreed to new levels of cooperation that will make it easier to uncover bribery, easier to follow the paper trail, and easier to get the money back. These "mutual legal assistance" provisions[5] require countries to provide assistance "to the fullest extent possible under relevant laws, treaties, agreements and arrangements . . . with respect to investigations, prosecutions and judicial proceedings" arising out of UNCAC offenses. This cooperation specifically includes taking evidence; serving court documents; conducting searches; providing documents, including government, bank and business records; tracing and freezing the proceeds of bribery for purposes of gathering evidence; and, ultimately, recovering assets. These sweeping provisions also include cooperation between the law enforcement agencies of different countries.[6] Together, these provisions help to ensure that relevant evidence can be collected across borders, regardless of the resources and political will of each country involved, and ultimately—at least ideally—be presented in one court for the best chance of a thorough review of the facts and, if appropriate, conviction.

Detracting from the procedural success story of the UNCAC is the concern that those accused of bribery of foreign officials may be subject to prosecution in multiple jurisdictions. There is no provision for "double jeopardy" under international law. If a company is based in one country, makes one payment to an agent in a second country, through a bank account in a third, for purposes of delivering a bribe to a government official in a fourth, the company is potentially subject to prosecution in all four countries for the single payment. This may strike some as heavy-handed. Before any wrongdoing is established, a company may have to fight court battles on multiple fronts with the expense, distraction, and damage to reputation that that entails. This concern is exacerbated by the fact that the courts of many countries are themselves susceptible to both political pressure and bribery. These concerns are likely to be addressed through negotiations over time; until they are, these UNCAC provisions increase the risk and potential cost to those engaged in bribery schemes and, as such, increase the deterrent value of the Convention.

As a practical matter, if a government official can be induced to publicly endorse a law that criminalizes bribery, regardless of what is in his heart, mind, or financial interests, he makes bribery more difficult for himself. Prior to the adoption of these conventions and the national laws they produced, a government official and whoever sought to bribe him could have had a reasonably open and moderately civilized conversation about the payment the official expected. These conversations took place, on rare occasions, quite openly in offices and at restaurants. While bribe negotiations certainly continue today, they tend to be more furtive. They have been forced into the darkened back corners of restaurants. They are rarely routine. This is reflected in the elaborate measures taken to obscure the paper trail: numbered or nominee bank accounts, front companies, offshore accounts in countries with little banking transparency, cash transactions that are difficult to trace, and payments to family members rather than to government officials directly.

Increasing the risk of discovery to either party to a corrupt transaction—to the one who offers or to the one who solicits—reduces the likelihood that they will successfully collude. If both parties are reluctant to raise the issue first, there is a chance that it won't get raised at all. If the corporate executive or commercial agent who might once have offered a cut to the government official freely now believes there is some risk that he will be prosecuted and potentially imprisoned at home or in a foreign country, he is likely to want to be sure that the person to whom he proposes a payment welcomes the idea. At the same time, while the overall risk remains lower for government officials, in the wake of the publicity surrounding recent new anti-bribery laws and penalties, they may also hesitate to raise the issue first.

ENFORCING THE LAW

One obvious measure to take to reduce bribery is to enforce the laws against it. Countries are beginning to be held accountable for failing to actively pursue bribery offenses. For instance, the procedures agreed to by the Working Group on Bribery of the OECD Convention require each country to be subjected to periodic reviews by other countries to evaluate and monitor the country's ongoing enforcement efforts and compliance with the Convention. Public recommendations are then made to the country to address shortcomings in its anti-bribery enforcement efforts. When the United Kingdom's Serious Fraud Office closed its investigation into the BAE Al Yamamah contract, for example, the decision was sharply rebuked by both the OECD and in a diplomatic communication from the U.S. Embassy in London.[7] On June 26, 2007, BAE announced that the U.S. Department of Justice has opened a formal investigation into the Al Yamamah allegations.

Even though there have been relatively few enforcement actions brought by governments to date, this much is clear: when a corporation is brought under investigation for bribery allegations, an extended disaster will ensue.

The investigation will mean a lengthy and expensive disruption of business as usual. Agents with yellow tape may arrive to seal off offices and filing rooms. Records and computers will be seized. Employees will be required to participate in detailed depositions and in the course of these proceedings divisive issues will arise among them. Individual employees may get word that they should seek "independent" counsel as their interests and the company's diverge. An investigation can be catastrophic for a corporation's morale and culture.

Legal fees for both the corporation and individual employees will mount over the years and may not end when the case is settled. Rather, they may climax in a stunning additional sum when, as has been the trend in recent cases, an independent compliance monitor is assigned to the company. One compliance monitor informed the company to which he was appointed with the approval of the U.S. Department of Justice that the company could expect his team's fees to reach US$30 million over the ensuing five years, provided the case did not develop further complications.

Legal fees may be minor in comparison to reputational damage and the loss attributable to diminished future earnings or spoiled opportunities for joint ventures or acquisition. In the Titan case, it was the preacquisition review that surfaced evidence of bribery. As a result, the buyout toward which the company's executives had worked was aborted.

Is a bribe-paying company likely to be caught? Several factors make it more likely. Its rivals tend to know when there are bidding irregularities on major deals, and those rivals have strong incentives to report them. Even if bribery during the bidding process can be concealed, and the bought official stays bought, there is the problem of covering up records of the payment. Bribe-paying entails accounting fraud, and as is the case in political corruption, it is often the paper trail of the cover up that leads to convictions.

The bribe-payer has put himself in the hands of the person he is paying off. The bribe-taker might be quite ready to offer the payer up to authorities. One can't know how he would behave, except that one can be sure he is not a person of high ethical standards. Similarly, a contractual dispute can make it more advantageous to admit involvement in a bribery scheme, rather than denying it, as we saw in the World Duty Free arbitration. A company might unexpectedly find itself with a publicly available record of its shady business practices.

How much impact could a few enforcement actions have? How many convictions would it take to clean up an industry? How many bribe-takers or payers must be caught before others will be constrained or deterred? It is difficult to say, since the answers would depend on many factors, including how great the payoff was to the bribe-givers and takers, how great the chance of being caught, and how dire the consequences if convicted. Though it is hard to account for these factors merely by speculating, they can be modeled quite successfully in computer simulations, and the outcomes are encouraging.

SEEING AROUND CORNERS

For about fifteen years, an economist named Thomas Schelling of Harvard and later the University of Maryland has been building computer models to capture such complex choices. He and Jason Epstein at the Brookings Institution created simulations in which artificial societies of agents or actors are assigned certain payoffs and penalties for their choices and then set free to interact. A protégé of Epstein's named Ross Hammond has refined their models and applied them specifically to bribe-taking and paying.

In Hammond's models, two kinds of agents he calls citizens and bureaucrats interact. In an adaptation of the classic "prisoner's dilemma," both actors do best if they trust one another and collaborate. In the context of this game, that means that they make an under-the-counter deal and the citizen buys the bureaucrat's influence. Both receive a substantial payoff. They do considerably worse if either one is honest. If one offers or solicits a bribe and the other refuses, the offeror or solicitor is punished with a report to the authorities. The agents are not allowed to know how many reports will earn them an arrest, which reflects the real enforcement climate in most countries.

Hammond set his digital agents to work playing the game, lacing the scene with a tiny number of "George Washingtons"—agents who are incorruptible and will never pay or accept a bribe. In every game, a surprising outcome occurred. Sometimes it was after a few minutes, sometimes after a few hours, but the same thing always occurred. Sooner or later, quite by accident, a few more agents than usual would be reported and the others would suddenly shape-up. That is to say, the reporting of a few extra offenders would cause a few extra arrests and the balance would suddenly skew toward honesty.

Jonathan Rauch explains the sudden change in an article in The Atlantic Monthly:[8]

> Every so often, in the course of random events, a particularly large num-
> ber of corrupt agents, who happen to have particularly large networks
> of friends who perhaps themselves have large social networks, will be
> arrested. That, Hammond figures, has a double-barreled effect: it leads a
> lot of agents to notice that many of their friends are under arrest, and it
> also increases the likelihood that they will encounter an honest agent in
> the next transaction. Fearing that they will meet their friends' fate, the
> agents behave more honestly; and in doing so they heighten yet further
> the odds that a corrupt agent will be nailed, inspiring still more cau-
> tion about corruption. Soon—in fact, almost instantly—so many agents
> are behaving honestly that corruption ceases to pay, and everyone turns
> honest.

The situation has "tipped," the simulation suggests. The model indicates that introducing unwanted consequences for a few key agents at a key moment can cause a major reversal in the prevalence of brib-ery. Subsequent variations in the model strongly suggested that unpre-dictability is important—that the behavior of the police should not be foreseeable. Binges of enforcement are most effective, and the behavior of other agents must be unpredictable as well. Fortunately, such unpre-dictability seems to be the prevailing condition in the real world.

One other encouraging element of the model: once the system "tipped," it stayed tipped. As Rauch puts it, "honesty is the new norm. With everybody behaving honestly, there is no payoff for corruption, (payoff requires two corrupt dealers), so the [artificial] society stays honest."

Schelling's experiments with agent-based modeling and artificial societies have drawn a good deal of attention in recent years. In 2006, he was awarded the Nobel Prize in economics.

INTERNATIONALIZING THE ISSUE

The sequence of anti-bribery conventions has finally accomplished the "internationalization" of the issue. For almost twenty years, the United States was the only country that made it a crime to bribe foreign officials, although U.S. corporate hands were by no means clean. That gave rise to resentment overseas of what was perceived as American determination to police the world, without first getting its own house in order. It also created resentment within the U.S. business com-munity where pressure to comply with the FCPA was thought to put U.S. companies at a disadvantage when their competitors were able to bribe with impunity and, in many cases, could expect the bribes to be subsidized by the state.[9] The UNCAC and its predecessor conventions ensured that, at least on paper, efforts to reduce bribery were no longer just a priority of the United States or of developed countries. For the first time, every party to a large bid—contractor, subcontractor, commercial agent, and customer—was bound, in theory, by similar rules.

SHINING THE SPOTLIGHT ON GOVERNMENT OFFICIALS

Once the UNCAC came into force, countries appeared to accept that their status on the international regulatory field would depend on reducing bribery, or appearing to take steps that would result in the reduction of bribery. The latter description is more appropriate in countries where government officials use anti-bribery campaigns as a political tool either to undermine their predecessors or to defame their opponents. Nigeria's former president, Obasanjo, accused his vice president and political nemesis, Abubakar, of involvement in bribery. Abubakar's response was to implicate Obasanjo. Recognizing that bribery introduces both a financial cost and a cost in time and aggravation—the "hassle factor"—many countries have been keen to impress the international community with their efforts to reduce bribery and so make their market more attractive to foreign investors. In 2006, in an effort to quash "rampant bribery," the little red envelopes of cash, *hong bao*, were outlawed for government officials in southern China.[10] The Guangdong provincial government announced that any Party member or government official who accepted *hong bao* would be removed from their post and might face prosecution.[11]

Dictators like Abacha, Marcos, Suharto, and Hussein typically store the money they extort or are paid in bribes in foreign accounts. Presumably, they do this in part to keep it out of the reach of successor governments, if any, and so it will be available to them should they need to flee. Dictators appear to spend a great deal of time diversifying in anticipation of a second career—voluntary or otherwise. Swiss banks are not the safe havens for criminal funds that they once were. In part because of the Swiss law enacted to comply with the OECD Convention, the Swiss authorities will now provide bank records if there is evidence that the account was used to hide or launder the proceeds of a crime. With this level of cooperation from all but a handful of banks and pressure on those still holding-out, there are few places left to hide the money.

There has been modest success repatriating money stolen directly from state treasuries or accumulated through bribery and self-dealing. In 2006, Swiss banks returned to Nigeria approximately US$700 million sitting in Abacha accounts.[12] This is a relatively small portion of the Abacha loot, but a considerable step forward. In 2003, the Swiss returned to the government of the Philippines approximately US$690 million of the roughly US$10 billion thought to have been stolen or extorted by former President Ferdinand Marcos.[13] If the estimates are correct, the money returned to date represents just 7 percent of the total that the family is still hiding, but the recovery of money no one in the Philippines expected to see again is nevertheless progress. And it seems that both parties can tire of the protracted litigation and elaborate financial shell games. Lawyers for Imelda Marcos have met with representatives of the Filipino government to discuss a possible settlement.[14] One senior official with the Presidential Commission on Good Government has reportedly asked Marcos's lawyer for a list of assets held by the family.[15] The Filipino government faces the same challenge that the Nigerian government must address: those with the best information about the amount of money and its whereabouts have the least incentive to disclose the information.

The Swiss government has frozen, but not yet returned, smaller amounts of money of questionable origin associated with former Haitian dictator Jean-Claude "Baby Doc" Duvalier and Mobutu Sese Seko, the former president of Zaire, now the Democratic Republic of the Congo.[16] To the extent that these and other dictators seek to secure their financial future and that of their families, this repatriation of looted funds must be disheartening. But, like Abacha and Marcos, Duvalier and Mobuto never stood trial for any of their crimes, financial or otherwise. This, too, is beginning to change.

The South Korean government has taken, at least sporadically, a hard line on this issue. President Cho'n Tu-hwan governed South Korea for eight years until he stepped down in 1988. Eight years later, in 1996, he was convicted of embezzlement and bribery and ordered to return 220 billion won (US$240 million). Tu-hwan was pardoned after spending just one year in jail, but in 2004 his son was indicted for tax evasion. It seems he didn't pay taxes on bonds valued at over seven billion won (US$7.5 million)—given to him by his father.[17]

Mr. Jacob Zuma had been a darling of South Africa's African National Congress. He was appointed in 1999 to the position of Deputy President by current president Thabo Mbeki and, in that position, was Mbeki's apparent heir. But in June 2005, Zuma's friend and financial adviser, Schabir Shaik, was convicted of corruption and fraud.[18] Among the crimes with which Shaik was charged was attempting to solicit a bribe for Zuma from a French defense company. The appellate court judges are reported to have found that payments made by Shaik "were corruptly made to influence Mr. Zuma to act in conflict with his constitutional duties."[19] Within days of Shaik's conviction, Zuma was removed as Deputy President.[20] On September 20, 2006, the case against Zuma himself was aborted, but he has not been reinstated and his career appears to have stalled.

Back in China, a country responsible for about 80 percent of the world's state-sponsored executions annually, government officials face the possibility of the death penalty for bribery. On February 12, 2004, Wang Huaizhong, a provincial vice governor, was executed for accepting US$600,000 in bribes[21] Media reports indicated that, when the investigation into the illegal payments began, Wang attempted to bribe the investigators to drop the case.[22] On July 10, 2007, China executed the former head of its Food and Drug Administration, Zheng Xiaoyu, although this seems to have been motivated more by a desire to restore confidence in Chinese food and drug safety standards than by the US$832,000 in bribes he was alleged to have accepted during his tenure.

In China, the death penalty is available to prosecutors for sixty-eight offenses, including cases of tax evasion, smuggling, and bribery.[23] While few would endorse the death penalty for financial crimes, this does demonstrate China's decision to send the strongest possible rebuke to bribe-takers. In democratic states, the voters are beginning to express their growing intolerance of bribery and those seeking election have responded, at least in their rhetoric.

Taiwan's Democratic Progressive Party (DPP) defeated the Chinese Nationalist Party (KMT) in both 2000 and 2004 by campaigning on an anti-corruption platform.[24] When the KMT won back a key mayoral post in Taipei in December 2006, the candidate declared that the election was one in which "the uncorrupt KMT defeats the corrupt DPP . . ."[25] In one poll in the United States, 51 percent of those who responded indicated that they believe political corruption in the United States to be a "very serious problem."[26]

In the web of international financial crimes, government officials can be removed from office for both receiving and giving bribes. In the tiny South Pacific nation of Tonga, former official Siosifa Fatafehi Fuataki-folaha was removed from his seat on the Tongan Legislative Assembly by the country's Supreme Court after he was found guilty of offering bribes to a Tongan customs officer.[27] Voters aren't reliable in this respect, however. In the United States, William J. Jefferson, the U.S. Congressman for Louisiana famously found with US$90,000 in his freezer, was reelected in 2006 in that state inspite of allegations of bribery in connection with as many as seven separate deals.[28] Jefferson was indicted on June 4, 2007, on federal charges of both soliciting and paying bribes.

CREATIVE RESPONSES FROM GOVERNMENT

In some cases, governments have shown great ingenuity in their attempts to reduce bribery. In 2002, the Colombian government launched an online procurement program that reduced state purchases to an anonymous, online bidding process for all but the most complicated or sensitive procurement decisions. By removing the personal exchanges surrounding these contracts and reducing them to anonymous technical descriptions and prices, the opportunity for bribery was also removed. The government of the Slovak Republic, recognizing the high level of bribery amongst Slovakian judges, automated case assignments so that judges could no longer select cases based on their lucrative nature or prior inappropriate contacts with the parties.

CONSEQUENCES FOR PRIVATE ACTORS

While government officials in many countries are just beginning to feel the impact of anti-bribery sentiment, citizens in the private sector have been feeling the pressure for several years. They feel the impact in extradition efforts, prosecution, fines and, in some cases, imprisonment. Saybolt North America Inc. is a testing and inspection company that supports the oil and gas industry. In 1998, the company was fined US$3.4 million and given a five-year probationary period for paying bribes in Panama. In addition to the company, two Saybolt executives were charged. One, Frerik Pluimers, was the CEO of Saybolt International. A resident of the Netherlands, Pluimers did not appear in court in the United States at the time of the trial. Presumably keen to avoid extradition, he reportedly has not left the Netherlands in the nine years since legal proceedings began. In the words of a Dutch lawyer who has followed the case: "nine years is a long time and Holland is a small, flat country."

Hans Bodmer, a Swiss lawyer, was initially implicated in Kozeny's Oily Rock scheme in Azerbaijan. Bodmer was indicted in the United States in 2003 for conspiracy to violate the U.S. foreign anti-bribery law and for conspiracy to launder money. Bodmer was arrested in South Korea while on business travel there. After spending five months in a South Korean prison,[29] he agreed to be extradited to the United States for trial. In 2004, his motion to dismiss the bribery charges was successful. He later pleaded guilty to conspiring to launder money and returned to Switzerland in November 2004, bringing his global ordeal to an end.[30]

Once in the legal system, at least in the United States, individuals face stiff penalties. In 2005, David Kay and Douglas Murphy, both former executives of American Rice Inc., were sentenced to thirty-seven months and sixty-three months in prison respectively.[31] These are the longest prison sentences to date for executives accused of paying bribes under the U.S. Foreign Corrupt Practices Act.[32] In July 2006, four former executives of Vetco Gray Ltd. settled charges with the SEC that they had bribed Nigerian officials without admitting the allegations. Together, they paid over US$230,000. In August 2006, David Pillor, the former Senior Vice President for Sales and Marketing for InVision

Technologies Inc., was charged with failing to establish adequate internal controls to prevent bribery of foreign government officials. Pillor settled, without admitting guilt, and paid a US$65,000 fine. Richard Novak and Blake Carlson of Liberian diploma mill fame paid fines totaling more than US$43,000.[33] In June 2006, Steven Lynwood Head, a former executive with Titan Corporation also pleaded guilty to falsifying the US$2 million invoice that is alleged to have generated the money to pay support to the reelection campaign of the then-president of Benin.[34] Recent patterns of fines for individual executives provide a deterrent to bribery by others,[35] especially in light of the requirement under U.S. law that the executives pay these fines themselves. The law prohibits companies from paying the fines on behalf of employees.

Outside the United States, the offices of electronics and engineering giant, Siemens, were raided in November 2006 and seven employees were taken into custody in an investigation into an alleged slush fund worth US$553 million.[36] If the arrests did not provide a strong enough disincentive to companies looking on, Finnish telecommunications company, Nokia, temporarily postponed its proposed joint venture with Siemens,worth approximately US$26 billion. While it is in no one's best interest to have havoc wrought with the international business community, executives respond to perceived risk. Few companies have the luxury of shareholders willing to invest in navigating international bribery shoals if there is no cost for non-compliance. Until a real risk of exposure and prosecution is perceived, few companies allocate staff and resources to protect their assets and their reputation.

PUTTING ANTI-BRIBERY COMPLIANCE ON THE BUSINESS AGENDA

In April 2006, CFO Magazine wrote about the eight top risks facing multinational companies.[37] Companies are worrying more, doing more, and spending more on anti-bribery compliance than at any time in the past. Some companies are taking the issue seriously as a part of a larger good corporate citizenship campaign, but most have made this a priority because enforcement agencies have made it a priority. They fear prosecution, quashed deals, plummeting share prices, vast fines, and jail time. True to the Schelling model, it takes just one or two executives escorted out of the courtroom in bright orange jumpsuits to capture the attention of the business world. In the last ten years, companies have formed anti-bribery "best practices" groups and defense, pharmaceutical, and financial services companies have established industry groups to benchmark practices that work and to share successful strategies.

Companies are cooperating on one issue in particular: ending the practice of making facilitating payments. Companies have grown tired of making these petty, extortionate payments for even the most basic services. Executives who travel almost constantly don't want anything to do with the risk and hassle that these payments introduce. They've had enough and, surprisingly, many company policies are now more restrictive than the law requires. Although expressly permitted under the FCPA, many companies prohibit facilitating payments except when an employee's safety or liberty is in jeopardy. In order to respond to the nearly constant demands in the most challenging markets, competitors are collaborating to roll out aggressive policies together on the theory that government officials can't hold them all hostage simultaneously. Companies that are otherwise cutthroat competitors are recognizing that, on the issue of bribery, they can minimize the "prisoners' dilemma" only by agreeing to play by the same rules. These agreements reflect a growing global conviction that bribery is wrong, but also that it is uneconomical, inefficient, costly, distorting of proper incentives and outcomes, risky, and generally unprofitable. It is, in short, a poor way to do business.

DOING THE RIGHT THING

It can be helpful to analyze bribery entirely as the tension between immediate, short-term self-interest—winning the contract, lining one's pocket—and fear of any number of consequences. But there are those who are speaking out against bribery simply because they sincerely believe bribery to be wrong. These anti-bribery advocates are found in some unexpected places and include some of the communities discussed in a less positive light in previous chapters.

The World Bank, after years of silence on this issue, has, through its Department of Institutional Integrity, launched a program to help deter and detect bribery on Bank projects. Recognizing that, just as in the early days of the FCPA, there was a backlog of bribe-tainted deals, the Voluntary Disclosure Program (VDP) was launched in August 2006, to offer confidentiality and clear and predictable benefits to those who step forward and "come clean" on past bribery. They must disclose past corrupt practices, commit not to engage in misconduct in the future, and implement a meaningful compliance program with oversight by a Bank-approved monitor. The disclosing person or entity bears the cost of the program, but can avoid debarment and adverse publicity for past misconduct and can continue to compete for Bank projects. Because the process of disclosing may well implicate competitors, government officials and others in the project supply chain and because the amnesty is not available to those already under investigation, the Bank expects companies to rush to report before someone else does it for them— turning the prisoners' dilemma to the advantage of the enforcers.

Similarly, although without the same enforcement capability, the United Nations added a tenth principle to its Global Compact: businesses should work against all forms of corruption, including extortion and bribery. The Global Compact is a partnership between six UN agencies and the private sector to promote more responsible corporate citizenship. Although cynics might argue that the UN should work on internal compliance first, reaching across traditional private sector-public sector divides can deliver a powerful joint message to the international community, even if the practice on the ground is imperfect. There is no valid reason why the UN cannot be cleaning up its own house as it encourages others to do the same.

Some NGOs are weaving the anti-bribery message into their larger mission. Many aid organizations have argued—quite understandably—that delivering food to those in desperate need is more important than anything else and that bribes to warlords or bandits along the way is a price worth paying to accomplish that mission. The risk associated with this decision is two-fold: NGOs are likely to be targeted specifically because of the urgent nature of their mission and financial support for NGOs is likely to wane if donors believe their funds will be siphoned-off in this way. But NGOs are beginning to place a higher priority on anti-bribery efforts, particularly after problems arose during relief efforts for victims of the Asian tsunami disaster and the devastating earthquakes in Pakistan.

Global Grassroots is a small nonprofit that teaches entrepreneurial skills to genocide survivors in Rwanda and provides a combination of modest grants and microloans to help launch small social enterprises. The majority of participants are war widows and most are HIV positive because of the widespread use of rape as a tool of war. With much else to worry about, Global Grassroots and its Rwandan community decided early on to incorporate an anti-bribery message into the program. The goal is to ensure sustainability of projects and not only because charity is not a satisfying or viable long-term solution. With margins counted in pennies, rather than dollars, losing anything to bribery would be too much. The more widely held view that bribery can be addressed *after* more urgent problems are resolved means it often isn't ever addressed—either programs fail because of high levels of bribery or programs succeed and some in positions of authority learn to profit from low levels of transparency.

The Extractive Industries Transparency Initiative (EITI) is a project launched by the UK's former prime minister, Tony Blair, in 2003, following strong pressure exerted by the Publish What You Pay coalition. It seeks to improve governance in resource-dependent countries through the simultaneous publication of audited figures for the tax, revenue, and royalty payments made by extractive companies to governments on the one hand, and the receipts these governments record in their accounts on the other. Supported by oil and gas and mining companies, as well as by civil society and the institutional investor community, the coalition supports the publication and verification of revenue associated with oil, gas, and mining.

It has been useful to have the different stakeholders cooperate in this effort because it gives companies, already under growing pressure to disclose information in violation of explicit confidentiality provisions in contracts, a vehicle to act to improve transparency. When these numbers are published, the citizens of resource-dependent countries can begin to insist on accountability which is just what many governments fear. As such, extractive companies recognized that they faced a choice between two equally unattractive options: either business-as-usual, with growing political and social instability fuelled by growing public awareness of resource-driven theft and corruption, or making disclosures that would put them at risk of losing business or of legal action for breach of contract. The "third way" was therefore to enlist the help of their own governments as well as their fiercest civil society critics to help persuade host countries to embrace new transparency standards. The goal is to ensure that companies are able to increase transparency without incurring unacceptable legal or commercial risks. The debate has been interesting to watch. When it costs honest players nothing to participate in this process, the only conclusion left to draw is that those who do not participate prefer opacity over transparency.

The investment community has, on occasion, acted against its short-term self-interest to take a stand on higher ground. When the United Kingdom's Serious Fraud Office terminated the investigation into allegations of bribery by BAE, the Financial Times reported what it described as this rare case of the forces of capitalism acting against their own interest.[38] In spite of the rise in BAE's share price—good news for investors—the manager of the UK's largest pension fund wrote to Prime Minister Tony Blair to complain about the damage the decision had done to efforts to improve international business practices. Karina Litvack, Head of Governance & Sustainable Investment, F&C Management Plc, added that "for long-term investors, bribery and corruption distort and destabilize markets, expose companies to legal liabilities and reputational damage, disadvantage non-corrupt companies and reduce transparency for investors seeking investment opportunities."[39]

The vaguely glamorous patina that once surrounded kleptocrats has also faded. The fascination we shared in the stories of Imelda Marcos' shoe collection, for example, and tales of private jets with solid gold fixtures, has given way to something much closer to contempt. Teodoro Nguema Obiang Mangu, eldest son of the president of Equatorial Guinea—oil-rich, but home to a population of desperately poor—bought a US$35 million Malibu mansion on his official annual salary of US$60,000.[40] Instead of the old star-struck admiration for theft on a grand scale, the journalist who reported the real estate transaction advised neighbors that, if Obiang showed up at the door asking to borrow some sugar, they shouldn't expect to get their cup back.

Individuals are saying "no" with greater frequency. While a simple "no" will not work in all, or even most, cases, it should be tried more often. A demand for a bribe is a request that the employee become an accomplice to a crime. It is often possible simply to pretend to fail to hear the demand. This tactic is underused, but great success is reported by those who try it. Few bribe-takers thrust out their hand and state their demands clearly. Instead, there is a language used between bribe-payers and bribe-takers that is understood by both. Bribe-takers ask if you're going to "take care of them," "smile on them," or buy them "dinner" or "tea." Sophisticated businessmen may pride themselves on understanding this language, when they would be more astute if they failed to understand. The bribe-taker hopes to avoid stating his demand clearly and many businessmen are willing to accommodate this preference. If, on the other hand, the response is a blank stare and clear failure to understand, the official must decide either to speak more plainly or to let this opportunity pass. Driving demands underground can itself be an effective strategy as it is easier to "fail to hear" demands that are very vague. Most officials will choose to let the opportunity pass and seek out easier prey.

Some blame the lawyers. When employees interacting with local officials on a regular basis decide to stop paying bribes, the change in policy can be difficult to explain to the beneficiaries of past largesse. As they must maintain good relations with many of these officials, it can be useful to have someone else to blame for the new policy. Employees can accurately attribute to those at headquarters the company's decision to stop all illegal payments. This position is given even greater weight when the employee is able to cite recent record-breaking fines for companies and extended prison sentences for executives who have been prosecuted for paying bribes.

Individuals can shine light on the problem. Although most companies are unwilling to draw much attention to demands for bribes, even to demands they resist, one very effective tactic is to have several companies report collectively on bribery "flashpoints." They may report bribe demands through an embassy if they have confidence that the information will be conveyed anonymously, or they may report through a neutral third party. The goal is to keep the companies' names out of any report to minimize soured relations—or even retaliation—while alerting the government officials that their behavior is being monitored. Most bribe-takers are risk-averse. If they believe someone is paying attention, they will be far less brazen in their approach.

While the private sector is working to reduce the payment of facilitating payments, too little attention is being paid to demand-side bribery.

There is currently little cost to the government officials who extort payments as an illegal tax on business. Real transparency would be enhanced by an international web-based reporting system through which corporations could report these demands anonymously. Companies know where many of the problems lie. Within every government, there are officials who are notorious for demanding their share and making trouble if it isn't forthcoming. Currently, companies do nothing with this information. They may decline to pay, but they're unlikely to risk alienating the government officials who are their customers.

TRACE is establishing such a reporting tool—publicly available and free of charge—through which companies will be able to report demands, voluntarily and anonymously. The information will not be used for prosecution. It will simply be collated and reported in the aggregate, by country and by government department: customs, defense, health, transportation, mining, etc. When these reports are published annually, they will alert government officials that their demands are being tracked. The information will not be used to intervene in individual transactions, but instead will be provided to governments to encourage remedial action and provided to companies as an additional tool in support of efforts to assess risk accurately.

Companies can send the bill to the local government partner, if there is one. One company in a joint venture with the state-owned oil company in a particularly challenging African country began sending the bill to its joint venture partner for half the cost of any delays resulting from a refusal to pay bribes. There were no accusations; there was no discussion of bribes at all. The bill simply stated that it was for expenses incurred as a result of delays in moving equipment. The equipment was delivered within two days and there were no future delays. It's important to note that bribe-taking government officials want to avoid embarrassment and confrontation. They'll stop stealing with their left hands if they must pay for it with their right.

To deal with the problem of false extra charges for "extra services," executives should find a legitimate mechanism by which they can pay for genuine additional services. Some executives have voiced the opinion that bribes are just a form of corporate tax and, after all, companies often strain local security and other services. This is true in many cases, but payments for legitimate services—overtime, work during local holidays, additional work generated by the company's need for expedited service—should be paid in a forthright way, not funneled through inappropriate channels. If real additional value is being provided, the company might consider proposing a formal arrangement whereby some of the expense is paid by the company under the terms of a transparent, documented agreement. Companies pay more for overnight delivery than they pay for regular mail. The key distinction is that the additional fee is not slipped to the delivery man, but is part of a published fee-for-service schedule.

Many people—in government, in business, in civil society, and private citizens—have had enough. They don't want to be a part of this criminal activity and they are ready to look at the issue anew and develop creative responses to the tiresome old routine. They know that bribery isn't glamorous, it isn't worldly and it isn't a sign of business sophistication. Companies' bribes paid to speed through customs and security look the same to the Moscow airport officials as those paid by suicide bombers. Corporate bribes paid on the casual advice of travel guides to the Guatemalan police look the same as those paid by narcotraffickers. In short, they look seamy, seedy, and illegal. Bribes often represent a corporate admission of defeat—a failure to think outside the box. When we pay bribes, we're complicit in our own extortion and we make it easy for those prepared to abuse their office and the public trust to enrich themselves.

There are many facile and convenient self-excusing rationalizations for participating in bribery. They are tired devices, these well-worn excuses for tolerating and joining in the undermining of the law and the legitimacy of a country. Surely this is the century in which the long-standing and ill-informed toleration of bribery will come to an end, the way the toleration of slavery came to end in the nineteenth century and the approval of trade in narcotics came to an end in the twentieth century. In this century, we will see once again the familiar pattern by which the popular mind comes to terms with a great change in tolerance of wrongdoing. For centuries there has been denial and disregard for a powerful idea like these—that the slave trade or the heroin trade or the pirate's trade is wrong. Then comes a time of turbulence in which the proponents of a higher standard will be mocked or abused or generally decried. Then, and we are approaching this point with the practice of bribery, there will come the mysterious tipping point when it will be clear to all concerned that profiting from the trade in people or from the exploitation of their addictions or from preying on undefended shipping is utterly and obviously wrong. Then, suddenly—and this is the most satisfying moment—all will simultaneously proclaim that the truth is self evident and was something they passionately believed all along. What right-thinking person could fail to see it? And then the change will have come. That moment is already near for the ancient and dishonorable practice of bribery. We will see it discredited in our lifetimes, and we will be more secure and more prosperous for its end.

Notes

Introduction: Thieves, Thugs, and Kleptocrats

1. NigeriaInvestment.com, "Abuja: The Tourist's Destination," http://www.nigeriainvestment.com/country/social/abuja.html.

2. Ibid.

3. Orji Ogbonnaya Orji, *Inside Aso Rock* (n.p.: Spectrum Books Ltd., 2003).

4. David Blair, "The vindictive military despot who stole billions," *Telegraph.co.uk*, June 25, 2005, http://www.telegraph.co.uk/news/main.jhtml?xml=/news/2005/06/25/wnig125.xml.

5. Media accounts differ as to which country in the Middle East Maryam Abacha intended to flee. A 1998 media account reported that Maryam Abacha was fleeing Nigeria for Saudi Arabia. In his May 2006 testimony before a committee of the U.S. Congress, George B.N. Ayittey testified that, shortly after General Abacha's death, local newspapers reported that Mrs. Abacha was thought to be headed to Lebanon. See George B.N. Ayittey, "Nigeria's Struggle with Corruption," Testimony before the Committee on International Relations' Subcommittee on Africa, Global Human Rights and International Operations House Sub-Committee on Africa, U.S. House of Representatives, May 18, 2006, 3, http://www.internationalrelations.house.gov/archives/109/ayi051806.pdf and Cameron Duodu (London Observer Service), "Late Dictator Bled Nigeria of Money Abacha and His Family Found to Have $750 Million in Foreign Cash so Far," *The Milwaukee Journal Sentinel*, sec. A, November 29, 1998.

6. Hari Sharan Chhabra, "Window on Africa: After Mobutu, it's Abacha," *The Tribune (India) Online*, December 17, 2000, http://www.tribuneindia.com/2000/20001217/world.htm.

7. Duodu, "Late Dictator Bled Nigeria of Money Abacha and His Family Found to Have $750 Million in Foreign Cash so Far."

8. Chhabra, "Window on Africa: After Mobutu, it's Abacha;" Paul Salopek, "Nigeria, At Last, Strikes at Corruption," *Chicago Tribune*, sec. News, September 8, 2000.

9. The Nigerian government reported that Abacha and his family stole US$4.3 billion in public funds during his time in power. BBC News, "Abacha Family Stole $4bn," February 8, 2000, http://news.bbc.co.uk/1/hi/world/africa/635720 .stm.

10. The Committee to Protect Journalists ("CPJ") named Abacha the press' worst enemy of 1998. CPJ is an independent, non-profit organization that promotes press freedom worldwide. The Committee to Protect Journalists, "Enemies of the Press: The Ten Worst Offenders of 1998," http://www.cpj .org/enemies/enemies1998.html. The current president of Nigeria, President Olusegun Obasanjo, was imprisoned by Abacha in 1995 for allegedly plotting a coup. Dan Isaacs, "Profile: Olusegun Obasanjo," *BBC News*, February 6, 2002, http://news.bbc.co.uk/2/hi/africa/1804940.stm. Kenule "Ken" Beeson Saro-Wiwa, an environmental activist, was hanged by military personnel on November 10, 1995. Amnesty International, "Nigeria: Ten years on: injustice and violence haunt the oil Delta," November 3, 2005, http://web.amnesty.org/ library/index/engafr440222005.

11. ThisDay (Nigeria), "Living in Limbo," April 22, 2005.

12. Lydia Polgreen, "As Nigeria Tries to Fight Graft, a New Sordid Tale," *New York Times*, sec. A, November 29, 2005.

13. BBC News, "Nigeria widows lose their fortune," September 7, 2006, http://news.bbc.co.uk/2/hi/africa/5325490.stm.

14. Duodu, "Late Dictator Bled Nigeria of Money Abacha and His Family Found to Have $750 Million in Foreign Cash so Far."

15. BBC News Online, "Switzerland to Give Back Abacha Millions," April 17, 2002, http://news.bbc.co.uk/2/hi/africa/1935646.stm.

16. AllAfrica.com, "Abacha Loot: Switzerland Returns $535m, Mohammed to Get Pardon," April 18, 2002.

17. Christina Lamb and David Wastell, "O.J. Lawyer to Defend Dictator's Family Over Stolen $8 Billion," *The Sunday Telegraph*, May 15, 2000. Johnnie Cochrane died on March 29, 2005, after being diagnosed with an inoperable brain tumor.

18. BBC News, "Abacha Family Stole $4bn."

19. Transparency International, *Global Corruption Report 2004* (London: Pluto Press, 2004), 13. Political corruption was the special focus of Transparency International's 2004 Global Corruption Report. Table 1.1 of the report contains a list of 10 alleged embezzlers, along with estimates of the amount of money they allegedly stole during their presidencies. Mohamed Suharto tops the list (US$15–$35 billion), followed by Ferdinand Marcos (US$5–$10 billion), Mobutu Sese Seko (US$5 billion) and Sani Abacha (US$2–$5 billion).

20. Estimates of Suharto's family fortune run anywhere from US$15 to US$35 billion. See Brendan I. Koerner, "How Did Suharto Steal $35 Billion?" March 26, 2004, http://www.slate.com/id/2097858/ and John Colmey and David Liebhold, "Suharto Inc.: The Family Firm," *TIMEasia.com*, May 24, 1999, http://www.time.com/time/asia/asia/magazine/1999/990524/cover1.html.

Chapter 1: Dimensions of Bribery

1. Amitav Ranjan, "Whistleblower said don't name me. Govt. did. He was shot dead." *The Sunday Express*, November 30, 2003. Satyendra Kumar Dubey,

an engineer on a large government infrastructure wrote to the Prime Minister's office to expose widespread corruption on the project. His request that his name not be associated with the report was ignored and he was murdered under suspicious circumstances.

2. Gregory Katz, "Nigeria bribery case heats up again," *Houston Chronicle*, sec. Business, November 12, 2006.

3. EFE Ingles, "Pinochet denies Hong Kong gold hoard is his," *EFE News Services (U.S.) Inc.*, October 25, 2006.

4. Katz, "Nigeria bribery case heats up again."

5. While technically a Constitutional Monarchy, many provisions of the constitution have been suspended since a State of Emergency was declared in 1962 and others were suspended after independence from the British in 1984.

6. Recounted to the author by the company's compliance officer, November 2005.

7. Recounted to the author at a TRACE Workshop in London, 2002.

8. Recounted to the author at in-house anti-bribery training, 2003.

9. Recounted to the author after a TRACE Workshop in Singapore, June 2005.

10. Katz, "Nigeria bribery case heats up again."

Chapter 2: The High Cost of Small Bribes

1. Ronald Noble, "Accountability of Political Leaders," Opening Plenary Session, 10th International Anti-Corruption Conference, Prague, Czech Republic, October 8, 2001, http://www.10iacc.org/content-ns.phtml?documents=500 &art=56.

2. Kim Murphy, "Russia May Pay for Bribes in Lives," *Los Angeles Times*, sec. Main News, November 8, 2004.

3. Ustinov, "Female Suicide Bomber Entered TU-154 for Bribe," *Interfax*, Russia & FSU News Bulletin (Daily News Briefs), September 15, 2004.

4. Murphy, "Russia May Pay for Bribes in Lives."

5. Ibid.

6. David McHugh, "Russia's Worst Enemy May be Its Own Police," *Associated Press*, September 11, 2004. The article quotes a Russky Kuryer newspaper account of a police report.

7. Ibid.

8. House Committee on Interstate and Foreign Commerce, *Unlawful Corporate Payments Act of 1977*, 95th Cong., 1st sess., 1977, H.R. Rep. No. 95-640, 4.

9. Senate Committee on Banking, Housing, and Urban Affairs, *Foreign Corrupt Practices and Domestic and Foreign Investment Improved Disclosure Acts of 1977*, 95th Cong., 1st sess., S. Rep. 95-114, 1977, 4.

10. The FCPA does not address domestic bribery, which is covered by other U.S. laws, including the Hobbs Act.

11. *SEC v. Syncor International Corporation* (D.D.C. 2002).

12. *United States v. Metcalf & Eddy* (D. Mass. 1999).

13. *United States v. James H. Giffen* (S.D.N.Y. 2003); *United States v. Viktor Kozeny, Frederic Bourke, Jr., and David Pinkerton* (S.D.N.Y. 2005); *SEC v. Titan Corporation* (D.D.C. 2005).

14. *United States v. James H. Giffen* (S.D.N.Y. 2003).

15. SEC Administrative Proceeding in the Matter of Schnitzer Steel Industries, Inc., October 16, 2006, File No. 3-12456.

16. *SEC v. Syncor International Corporation* (D.D.C. 2002).

17. *United States v. Titan Corporation* (S.D. Cal. 2005); *SEC v. Titan Corporation* (D.D.C. 2005).

18. *SEC v. Schering-Plough Corporation* (D.D.C. 2004); SEC Administrative Proceeding in the Matter of Schering-Plough Corporation, June 9, 2004, File No. 3-11517.

19. *The Foreign Corrupt Practices Act*, Public Law 105-366, codified at U.S. Code 15, § 78dd–1(a)(3).

20. *The Foreign Corrupt Practices Act*, Public Law 105-366, codified at U.S. Code 15, § 78dd–1(f)(2).

21. *The Foreign Corrupt Practices Act*, Public Law 105-366, codified at U.S. Code 15, § 78dd–1(b).

22. As defined in Robert Klitgaard, *Controlling Corruption* (Berkeley: University of California Press, 1988).

23. John T. Noonan, Jr., *Bribes* (New York: Macmillan, 1984), 696.

24. Four small and medium-sized companies complained to the author during research for *The High Cost of Small Bribes*, a TRACE publication, that they face more demands for facilitating payments than their colleagues at large companies and have less support and fewer resources with which to resist.

25. TRACE works with companies in several time-sensitive industries, including expedited delivery service companies, and two have recounted to the author schemes which reflect the bribe-demanders thorough (and cynical) understanding of the importance of timeliness to the companies' reputation.

26. Recounted to the author after a TRACE Workshop in Singapore, June 2005.

27. Recounted to the author by her driver during a one-year posting to Syria.

28. Energy Information Administration, "Top World Oil Net Exporters, 2005," http://www.eia.doe.gov/emeu/cabs/topworldtables1_2.html.

29. Discussion between the author and a Nigerian businessman during a TRACE Workshop about the latter's desire to set himself apart from his countrymen in order to establish a reputation as an honest and ethical businessman, February 2006.

30. dpa International Services in English, "Jet bomb plot: Police union criticises German airport security," *dpa Deutsche Presse-Agentur GmbH*, November 21, 2006.

31. *United States v. David Kay and Douglas Murphy* (S.D. Tex. 2002); *United States v. David Kay and Douglas Murphy* (5th Cir. 2004); *SEC v. Douglas A. Murphy, David G. Kay and Lawrence H. Theriot* (S.D. Tex. 2002).

32. Martin Weinstein, Partner, Willkie Farr & Gallagher LLP, remarks at the 2006 TRACE Forum, Washington, D.C., September 21, 2006.

33. *United States v. David Kay and Douglas Murphy* (S.D. Tex. 2002).

34. *United States v. David Kay and Douglas Murphy* (5th Cir. 2004).

35. Daniel Kaufmann and Shan-Jin Wei, "Does 'Grease Money' Speed up the Wheels of Commerce?" Paper presented at the American Economic Association Meeting, Chicago, IL, 1998.

36. Recounted to the author during the first of two TRACE Workshops in Moscow, November 2002.

37. Daniel Kaufmann, "Corruption: The Facts," *Foreign Policy*, Summer 1997.

38. Recounted to the author by a representative of an oil and gas company active in West Africa.

39. Recounted to the author during research for *The High Cost of Small Bribes*.

40. The National Border Patrol Museum, "U.S. Border Patrol Agents Killed in the Line of Duty," http://www.borderpatrolmuseum.com/2003memorial/complete.htm.

41. AP Alert, "Customs agent pleads guilty to drug smuggling charge," *The Associated Press*, October 27, 2006.

42. U.S. Department of Justice, "Rio Grand City Police Officers Convicted of Accepting Bribes," March 31, 2006, http://houston.fbi.gov/dojpressrel/pressrel06/ho033106b.htm.

43. U.S. Department of Justice, "Four Current and Former U.S. Soldiers Agree to Plead Guilty to Participating in Bribery and Extortion Conspiracy," March 9, 2006, http://www.usdoj.gov/criminal/pr/press_releases/2006/03/2006_4499_3-8-06LivelyGreen2.pdf.

44. Ibid.

45. U.S. Department of Justice, "Federal Air Marshals Convicted of Bribery and Drug Possession," April 3, 2006, http://houston.fbi.gov/dojpressrel/pressrel06/ho04032006.htm.

46. Leta Hong Fincher, "China-Army Corruption," *Voice of America* (Correspondence Report), July 19, 2000, www.fas.org/news/china/2000/000719-prc1.htm.

47. Willy Wo-Lap Lam, "How China Retreats to Attack," *CNN.com*, May 15, 2001, http://archives.cnn.com/2001/WORLD/asiapcf/east/05/15/china.willy.column/index.html.

48. Emma Poole, "U.S. Immigration Officer Pleads Guilty in Bribery Case," *The Calgary Herald*, July 26, 2002.

49. *R. v. Garcia*, 2002 ABPC 156 (CanLII).

50. The National Automated Immigration Lookout System (NAILS) "contains names and reference data on violators, alleged violators, and suspected violators of the criminal or civil provisions of the statutes enforced by INS, and other Federal law enforcement agencies. The system also maintains the name and reference data on persons not entitled to be admitted into the United States." U.S. Citizenship and Immigration Services, "Electronic Reading Room System Notice for National Automated Immigration Lookout System (NAILS)," Justice/INS-032.

51. Siskind's Immigration Bulletin, February 14, 2003, 18, http://www.visalaw.com/03feb2/newsletter.pdf.

52. United States Attorney Roslynn R. Mauskopf, Eastern District of New York, "Eight Defendants Arrested by the FBI and Charged with Conspiring to Provide Material Support and Resources to a Foreign Terrorist Organization and Related Offenses," August 21, 2006, http://www.usdoj.gov/usao/nye/pr/2006/2006Aug21.htm.

53. Adrian Humphreys, "Bribe money in Tamil terror case originated from Montreal, FBI allege," *CanWest News Service*, August 25, 2006, http://www.canada.com/nationalpost/news/story.html?id=f14acf77-3dbf-4aca-bf58-8f1e7c77a8f2&k=52933.

54. U.S. Attorney's Office Eastern District of Virginia, "Citizenship and Immigration Services Official Pleads Guilty to Bribery and Naturalization Fraud," November 30, 2006, http://www.usdoj.gov/usao/vae/Pressreleases/11-NovemberPDFArchive/06/20061130schofield_robertnr.pdf.

55. U.S. Attorney's Office Eastern District of Virginia, "Citizenship and Immigration Services Supervisor Sentenced for Bribery and Naturalization Fraud," April 20, 2007, http://www.usdoj.gov/usao/vae/Pressreleases/04-AprilPDFArchive/07/20070420schofieldnr.pdf.

56. George W. Grayson, "Unchanging Mexico," *San Diego Union-Tribune*, sec. Opinion, December 14, 2003.

57. John Pomfret, "Bribery at Border Worries Officials," *The Washington Post*, sec. A, July 15, 2006.

58. Ibid.

59. U.S. Customs and Border Protection, "President Bush's FY 2007 Budget for U.S. Customs and Border Protection (CBP) Totals $7.8 Billion," February 7, 2006, http://www.cbp.gov/xp/cgov/newsroom/fact_sheets/budget/bush_2007_budget.xml.

60. Pauline Arrillaga, "Corruption: How to secure homeland if some guardians have turned?" *AP Alert*, September 23, 2006.

Chapter 3: Gifts, Favors, and Hospitality

1. Noonan, Jr., *Bribes*, 695.

2. Susan Rose-Ackerman, *Corruption and Government: Causes, Consequences, and Reform* (Cambridge: Cambridge University Press, 1999), 92.

3. For a detailed discussion of the U.S. case law on the requisite standard of an inappropriate exchange with a government official and the distinction between a bribe and an illegal gratuity, see *United States v. Sun-Diamond Growers*, 138 F.3d 961 (D.C.Cir. 1998) aff'd, 526 U.S. 398 (1999).

4. Noonan, Jr., *Bribes*, 662. For a fascinating and detailed account of the Church Hearings, see pages 658–663. Prince Bernhard subsequently accepted the report of an official investigation and conceded that he had accepted US$1 million from Lockheed.

5. "In Asian countries, for instance, refusing a gift is often considered unspeakably rude. And in some less developed nations, foreigners are sometimes expected to "pay to play."" G. Jeffrey MacDonald, "When does a gift become a bribe?" *Christian Science Monitor* (January 25, 2006), http://www.csmonitor.com/2006/0125/p13s01-lire.htm.

6. Recounted to the author during research on TRACE Guidelines for Gifts and Hospitality.

7. In a 2005 interview, Peter Clark, former deputy chief of the U.S. Department of Justice Criminal Division's Fraud Section, recalled a company that sought approval to give a solid gold model airplane to a government official as a gift. Michael Goldhaber, "Mr. Clean," *American Law Journal* 27, no. 4 (April 2005).

8. The purchase of a Rolls-Royce for former Congressman Duke Cunningham is among the bribery, fraud, and tax evasion conspiracy described in court documents. See Office of the United States Attorney, Southern District of

California, "Former Congressman Cunningham Sentenced to More than 8 Years in Prison," March 3, 2006, http://www.usdoj.gov/usao/cas/press/cas60303-1.pdf.

9. U.S. prosecutors allege that fur coats are among the items purchased with millions of dollars in bribes channeled from James Giffen, a U.S. merchant banker indicted on foreign bribery charges, to top officials in the Kazakh government. Ron Stodghill, "Trial to put spotlight on U.S. support for Kazakhstan," *International Herald Tribune*, Issue 3, sec. Finance, November 7, 2006.

10. The 2003 indictment of James Giffen on charges of making more than US$78 million in unlawful payments to two senior officials of the Kazakh government alleged that one of the officials used the illegal funds provided by Giffen to pay for, among other things, tuition for his daughter to attend an exclusive high school. United States Attorney, Southern District of New York, "American Businessman Charged with $78 Million in Unlawful Payments to Kazakh Officials in 6 Oil Transactions; Former Mobil Corp. Executive Indicted for Tax Evasion in Kickback Scheme," April 2, 2003, 4, http://www.usdoj.gov/usao/nys/pressreleases/April03/giffenwilliams.pdf.

11. Recounted to the author at a meeting in Damascus, 1999.

12. Recounted to the author at a TRACE Workshop in Dubai, November 2006.

13. Recounted during discussions at a TRACE Workshop in Shanghai, May 2005.

14. Qin Jize, "Cakes take the bite of packaging," *China Daily*, September 28, 2004, http://www.chinadaily.com.cn/english/doc/2004-09/28/content_378205.htm.

15. Ibid.

16. Recounted to the author at a TRACE Workshop in Shanghai, March 2005.

17. Craig Timberg, "Nigerian Militants Destroy 3 Pipelines in Oil-Rich Delta: Raids a 'Warning' to President Elect," *The Washington Post*, May 9, 2007.

18. Peter Elkind, "The Incredible Half-Billion-Dollar Azerbaijani Oil Swindle Wherein we learn why smart players like Leon Cooperman, George Mitchell, and AIG would entrust buckets of their money to Victor Kozeny, a.k.a. the Pirate of Prague. (Hint: Can you say 'greed'?)," *Fortune Magazine* (March 6, 2000), http://money.cnn.com/magazines/fortune/fortune_archive/2000/03/06/275250/index.htm.

19. *United States v. Viktor Kozeny, Frederic Bourke, Jr., and David Pinkerton* (S.D.N.Y. 2005), Indictment, http://www.usdoj.gov/usao/nys/pressreleases/October05/kozenyetalindictment.pdf.

20. Ibid.

21. Recounted to the author at a TRACE Workshop in London, October 2004. A similar story was reported in the *Sunday Telegraph (UK)* in May 2005. It's difficult to know whether the second was an urban legend growing out of the first or whether the similarities are coincidental. The imaginations of briber-takers must, after all, have some limits.

22. See Stephen Wrage and Alexandra Wrage, "Multinational Enterprises as 'Moral Entrepreneurs' in a Global Prohibition Regime against Corruption," *International Studies Perspectives* 6, no. 3 (August 2005).

23. Recounted to the author after a TRACE Workshop in Sana'a, January 2006.

24. *United States v. Titan Corporation* (S.D. Cal. 2005); *SEC v. Titan Corporation* (D.D.C. 2005).

25. *SEC v. Schering-Plough Corporation* (D.D.C. 2004); SEC Administrative Proceeding in the Matter of Schering-Plough Corporation, June 9, 2004, File No. 3-11517; SEC Administrative Proceeding in the Matter of Statoil, ASA, October 13, 2006, File No. 3-12453.

26. The representative of a major multinational recounted to the author a request from an Indonesian customer that the multinational make a substantial donation to a disaster relief fund that turned out to be registered in the name of the president's wife.

27. U.S. Department of Commerce, Bureau of Industry and Security, "Offsets in Defense Trade 1999," http://www.bis.doc.gov/defenseindustrialbaseprograms/OSIES/offsets/offsetsdeftradeyr99v2.htm.

28. Recounted to the author in 1999 and 2002 by U.S. executives operating in the Middle East and Asia, respectively.

29. Recounted to the author in 1999 by a U.S. executive involved in the negotiations.

30. Recounted to the author by an executive with an American company in 2001.

Chapter 4: Undermining Confidence in Government

1. William Reno, "Political Networks in a Failing State: The Roots and Future of Violent Conflict in Sierra Leone," *Internationale Politik und Gesellschaft* 2 (2003): 60.

2. U.S. Department of Justice, "Army Reserve Officer Pleads Guilty to Money Laundering Conspiracy Involving Stolen Currency and Fraud in Iraq," August 25, 2006, http://www.usdoj.gov/criminal/press_room/press_releases/2006_4732_08-25-06iraqhopfengardner.pdf.

3. Special Inspector General for Iraq Reconstruction, "Quarterly Report to the United States Congress," October 30, 2006, J-4.

4. *United States v. Darleen A. Druyun* (E.D. Va. 2004), Supplemental Statement of Facts, 2.

5. Stephen J. Hedges, "Former U.S. Air Force Official Pleads Guilty in Boeing Tanker Deal Case," *Chicago Tribune (KRT)*, April 21, 2004.

6. *United States v. Darleen A. Druyun* (E.D. Va. 2004), Supplemental Statement of Facts, 2-3.

7. Ibid, 3.

8. Ibid, 2.

9. Agence France-Presse, "Former Pentagon official hired by Boeing pleads to conspiracy charge," April 20, 2004.

10. Tim Weiner, "Ex-Boeing Financial Chief Pleads Guilty to Felony," *New York Times*, November 16, 2004.

11. Stockholm International Peace Research Institute (SIPRI), SIPRI Military Expenditure Database, http://forst.sipri.org/non_first/milex.php.

12. TRACE International, Inc., *TRACE Survey of Corporate Anti-Bribery Programs 2004* (Washington, DC: TRACE International, Inc., 2004).

13. David Leppard, "Bid to end Saudi probe to safeguard arms deal," *Sunday Times (UK)*, sec. Home news, March 26, 2006; Isabel Oakeshott and David Leppard, "Leant on and lumbered - how Goldsmith 'put the state before the law'." *Sunday Times (UK)*, December 17, 2006.

14. Leppard, "Bid to end Saudi probe to safeguard arms deal."

15. David Leppard, "Blair hit by Saudi 'bribery' threat," *The Sunday Times*, November 19, 2006, http://www.timesonline.co.uk/article/0,,2087-2459780. html.

16. BBC News, "Timeline: BAE corruption probe," January 7, 2007, http:// news.bbc.co.uk/2/hi/business/6182137.stm.

17. Dominic O'Connell, "BAE cashes in on £40bn Arab jet deal," *The Sunday Times*, sec. News International, August 20, 2006.

18. Leppard, "Blair hit by Saudi 'bribery' threat;" Tom Regan, "Saudi Arabia threatens to suspend relations with Britain over bribery investigation," *Christian Science Monitor* (November 21, 2006), http://www.csmonitor.com/2006/1121/ dailyUpdate.html?s=rel.

19. Leppard, "Blair hit by Saudi 'bribery' threat."

20. Kenneth E. Sharpe, "THE DRUG WAR: U.S. Policy Corrupting Mexico Army," *Los Angeles Times*, August 10, 1997.

21. Eva Bertram and Kenneth E. Sharpe, *Drug War Politics, The Price of Denial* (Berkeley: University of California Press, 1996): 17.

22. Carlos Fazio, "Mexico: The Narco General Case," in *Crime in Uniform: Corruption and Impunity in Latin America* (Cedib: TNI and Acción Andina, 1997), www.tni.org/reports/drugs/folder3/fazio.htm. In this article, U.S. Director of the Office of National Drug Control Policy, Barry McCaffrey, is quoted as describing General Jesus Gutiérrez Rebollo as "a man with a reputation for impeccable integrity."

23. Ioan Grillo (Associated Press), "Jailed Mexican drug czar faces additional charges," *SignonSanDiego.com*, November 1, 2006, http://www.signonsandiego .com/news/mexico/20061101-1316-mexico-jaileddrugczar.html.

24. National Drug Strategy Network, "Mexican Drug Czar Fired, Charged with Drug Corruption," March-April 1997, http://ndsn.org/marapr97/drugczar.html.

25. Yale Global Online, "Avian Flu - Special Report on YaleGlobal," http:// yaleglobal.yale.edu/reports/avianflu.jsp.

26. Newt Gingrich and Robert Egged, "To Fight the Flu, Change How Government Works," *New York Times*, November 6, 2005.

27. Eithne Donnellan, "Expert criticises HSE's pandemic plan," *Irish Times*, sec. Health, May 23, 2006.

28. Centers for Disease Control and Prevention, "Key Facts About Avian Influenza (Bird Flu) and Avian Influenza A (H5N1) Virus," June 30, 2006, http:// www.cdc.gov/flu/avian/gen-info/facts.htm.

29. Donald G. McNeil Jr., "A few good killers sought for UN's war on bird flu," *International Herald Tribune*, January 30, 2006.

30. Ibid.

31. According to the National Institute of Allergy and Infectious Diseases, "[m]igratory birds, the poultry trade, and human travel are among the possible mechanisms that experts believe could introduce pandemic flu into the United States. Public health officials are monitoring these and other possible mechanisms as priorities for the health of the nation." National Institute of Allergy

and Infectious Diseases, "Questions and Answers: Avian Influenza Trials," February 2007, http://www3.niaid.nih.gov/news/QA/H5N1QandA.htm.

32. World News Connection, "Russia Focus -- Thematic Highlights from the Press and Internet for 31 Jan 06," January 31, 2006.

33. Laurie Garrett, *Betrayal of Trust: The Collapse of Global Public Health* (New York: Hyperion, 2000), 59.

34. Ibid, 115.

35. Maureen Lewis, "Rx for Corruption," *Foreign Policy*, July/August 2006.

36. Hindustan Times, "Setback for fight against dengue," October 7, 2006.

37. Ibid.

38. He Huifeng, "Guangzhou SARS hero admits bribery charges," *South China Morning Post*, October 12, 2006.

39. Ibid.

40. Ibid.

41. Emerald Dong, "Beijing health officials caught in bribery net," *South China Morning Post*, November 7, 2006; BBC International Reports (Asia), "Chinese health official investigated for taking bribe during SARS in 2003," *BBC Monitoring Service*, November 6, 2006.

42. Leu Siew Ying, "Sars hero sentenced to life in prison," *South China Morning Post*, September 2, 2006.

43. Ibid.

44. Recounted to the author during an ABA Section on International Law panel on NGOs and anti-bribery compliance, Washington, DC.

45. Associated Press, "Bad blood infects 63 Kazakh kids with HIV," *MSNBC*, September 28, 2006, http://www.msnbc.msn.com/id/15049613/.

46. The World Bank, *Global Monitoring Report 2006* (Washington, DC: The International Bank for Reconstruction and Development / The World Bank, 2006), 64.

47. World News Connection, "CIS: Epidemiology, Public Health Update on HIV/AIDS for 9-15 October," October 16, 2006. The observer quoted in this story is Torekhan Aday, identified in the news report as "a special prosecutor and senior assistant to the general public prosecutor of the Republic of Kazakhstan."

48. See The Pew Research Center for the People and the Press, "Broad Opposition to Genetically Modified Foods," Commentary, June 20, 2003, http://people-press.org/commentary/display.php3?AnalysisID=66.

49. U.S. Department of Justice, "Monsanto Company Charged with Bribing Indonesian Government Official: Prosecution Deferred for Three Years," January 6, 2005, http://www.usdoj.gov/criminal/press_room/press_releases/2005_3753_MONSANTO_COMPANY_CHARGED_WITH_BRIBING_INDONESIAN_GOVERNMENT_OFFICIAL_PROSECUTION_DEFERRED_FOR_THREE_YEARS.htm.

50. *SEC v. Monsanto Company* (D.D.C. 2005), Complaint, January 2005, par. 13, http://www.sec.gov/litigation/complaints/comp19023.pdf.

51. U.S. Department of Justice, "Monsanto Company Charged with Bribing Indonesian Government Official: Prosecution Deferred for Three Years."

52. There is a case with similar facts arising out of the conspiracy of employees at the Costa Rican subsidiary of Kansas City-based Owl Securities and Investment Ltd. to pay US$1.5 million to Costa Rican government officials to

secure changes to Costa Rican law that would make it simplify the company's land development project. *United States v. Halford*, 01 Cr. No. 221 (W.D. Mo. 2001); *United States v. Reitz*, 01 Cr. No. 222 (W.D. Mo. 2001); *United States v. Robert Richard King and Pablo Barquero Hernandez*, Cr. No. 01-190 (W.D. Mo. 2001).

53. AP Alert, "Former governor, seven others, receive long jail terms for illegal logging in Cambodia," *The Associated Press*, November 23, 2006.

54. dpa International Services in English, "Cambodia sentences powerful officials to jail for illegal logging," November 24, 2006.

55. AP Alert, "Former governor, seven others, receive long jail terms for illegal logging in Cambodia."

56. According to the Rainforest Foundation, "Indonesia is the world's largest exporter of tropical wood, but more than half of the country's timber production is illegal." The Rainforest Foundation, "Indonesia," http://www .rainforestfoundationuk.org/s-Indonesia?highlight=Indonesia.

57. Ioannis Gatsiounis, "Lenders seek ways to save Southeast Asian forests," *International Herald Tribune*, December 17, 2005.

58. New Zealand Ministry of Agriculture and Forestry, "New Zealand's First Interpol Conference: Wildlife Smuggling," Media Release, October 13, 2003, http://www.maf.govt.nz/mafnet/press/131003interpol.htm.

59. Ken Moritsugu, "India tiger preserve has lost all its tigers," *Albany Times Union*, May 22, 2005.

60. AP Asia, "Indian police arrest poacher for alleged involvement in disappearance of tiger," *The Associated Press*, June 30, 2005.

61. Moritsugu, "India tiger preserve has lost all its tigers."

62. Franz Wild, "Ivory Coast blames corrupt, negligent officials for toxic waste scandal," *The Associated Press*, November 23, 2006.

63. Ibid.

64. Ibid.

65. AP Online, "Top Egyptian archeologists to stand trial for smuggling thousands of antiquity pieces," *The Associated Press*, December 13, 2004.

66. Agence France-Presse, "No holiday 'red envelope' bribery for officials in southern China," September 28, 2006.

67. World News Connection, "County Official in Hubei Sentenced To Life for Embezzling Social Security Funds," November 27, 2006.

68. World News Connection, "Former Tangxia Township Head Jailed for Gambling Away Public Funds (Xinhua)," November 24, 2006.

69. Stephanie Nolen, "AFRICA ON THE BRINK: Part Three; Vanishing grain yield trips up attempts at renewal" *Globe and Mail*, sec. International News, June 18, 2002.

70. BBC News, "Malawi closes net on grain scam," *BBC News Online (news .bbc.co.uk)*, August 2, 2002, http://news.bbc.co.uk/1/hi/business/2168225 .stm.

71. Larry M. Edwards, "Titan Shares Skyrocket on Lockheed Acquisition," *SanDiego.com*, September 13, 2003, http://www.sandiego.com/sdbusiness .jsp?id=143.

72. In a 1977 House Committee Report, Lockheed is named three times in the discussion on how bribery creates foreign policy problems for the United States: ". . .For example, in 1976, the Lockheed scandal shook the

government of Japan to its political foundation and gave opponents of close ties between the United States and Japan an effective weapon with which to drive a wedge between the two nations. In another instance, Prince Bernhardt of the Netherlands was forced to resign from his official position as a result of an inquiry into allegations that he received $1 million in pay-offs from Lockheed. In Italy, alleged payments by Lockheed, Exxon, Mobil Oil, and other corporations to officials of the Italian government eroded public support for that government and jeopardized U.S. foreign policy, not only with respect to Italy and the Mediterranean area, but with respect to the entire NATO alliance as well." House Committee on Interstate and Foreign Commerce, *Unlawful Corporate Payments Act of 1977*, 95th Cong., 1st sess., 1977, H.R. Rep. No. 95-640, 5.

73. *United States v. Lockheed Corp.* (N.D. Ga. 1994); *United States v. Love* (N.D. Ga. 1994); *United States v. Nassar* (N.D. Ga. 1994).

74. *SEC v. The Titan Corporation* (D.D.C. 2005), Complaint, March 1, 2005, par. 35, http://www.sec.gov/litigation/complaints/comp19107.pdf.

75. Ibid, par. 17, 37-38.

76. Ibid, par. 72-81.

77. After the investigation began, Lockheed reduced its offer price to US$1.7 billion. Bruce Bigelow, "Iraq: Titan's Army contract under review," *San Diego Union-Tribune*, May 27, 2004.

78. Shortly after the Titan case became public, TRACE and the partner firms with which it works noted a dramatic upswing in interest in anti-bribery compliance tools. Membership in TRACE, a non-profit membership association that provides anti-bribery compliance solutions, doubled that year.

79. Integrated Regional Information Networks (IRIN), "BENIN: Smuggling, corruption and another term for the president," April 18, 2005, http://www .irinnews.org/S_report.asp?ReportID=46679&SelectRegion=West_Africa.

80. *United States v. Kenny Int'l Corp.*, Cr. No. 79-372 (D.D.C. 1979).

81. *United States v. Kenny Int'l Corp.*, Cr. No. 79-372 (D.D.C. 1979), Transcript of Proceedings, August 2, 1979.

82. Brian Ross, "From Cash to Yachts: Congressman's Bribe Menu," *ABC News Online*, February 27, 2006, http://abcnews.go.com/Politics/story?id=1667009& page=1.

83. Office of the United States Attorney, Southern District of California, "Former Congressman Cunningham Sentenced to More than 8 Years in Prison."

84. *United States v. Randall Harold Cunningham* (S.D. Cal. 2005), Information, November 28, 2005.

85. Toby Eckert and Jerry Kammer, "Report: Millions steered to contractors Intelligence panel's inquiry details abuses," *San Diego Union-Tribune*, October 18, 2006.

86. Associated Press, "Ex-congressman begins prison sentence," *MSNBC*, March 4, 2006, http://www.msnbc.msn.com/id/11655893/.

87. See, for example, Jonathan Ansfield, "China: Who Will Succeed Hu?" *Newsweek International*, October 9, 2006.

88. BBC News, "Nigeria governors in graft probe," *BBC News Online (news .bbc.co.uk)*, September 28, 2006, http://news.bbc.co.uk/2/hi/africa/5387814.stm.

89. World News Connection, "Nigeria: Vice President Abubakar Formally Declares To Run in 2007 Poll (AFP)," November 25, 2006.

90. Emmanuel Aziken, "Abacha is a Saint Compared to Obasanjo – Atiku," *AllAfrica.com*, January 29, 2007.

91. AP Alert, "Ex-president of top Chinese university dismissed from legislative body," *The Associated Press*, November 22, 2006.

92. Hindustan Times, "Judging the judges," November 24, 2006.

93. Volt Contreras, "SWS: Half of Lawyers Say Judges Accept Bribes," *Philippine Daily Inquirer*, August 26, 2005.

94. Recounted to the author by an Indonesian lawyer, August 1998.

95. Bruce Horowitz of PAZ HOROWITZ, Abogados, Quito, Ecuador.

96. North Country Gazette, "Judges, Attorney Convicted in Case Fixing, Bribery Scheme," April 2, 2007, http://www.northcountrygazette.org/articles/2007/040207CaseFixing.html.

97. 18 U.S.C. § 1346 (2006).

Chapter 5: Distorting Business

1. Thomas Catan and Joshua Chaffin, "Bribery has long been used to land international contracts. New laws will make that tougher." *FT.com*, May 8, 2003.

2. Prior to the criminalization of bribery in Europe in the late 1990s, bribes were not illegal and so were in fact deductible as a business expense.

3. *SEC v. GE InVision, Inc.* (N.D. Cal. 2005).

4. When asked by the author whether he believed in a commercial level playing field, a senior representative of a Scandinavian company responded that "with the scale of U.S. operations in [its industry] and the U.S. diplomatic pressure brought to bear on foreign government, [non-U.S. companies] have to pay bribes *in order to* level the playing field." Recounted to the author at a TRACE Workshop in Brussels, 2005.

5. Larry M. Edwards, "Titan Downplays SEC Probe, Merger on Schedule," *SanDiego.com*, February 13, 2004, http://www.sandiego.com/sdbusiness.jsp?id=235.

6. Associated Press, "Lockheed ends planned $1.66B deal with Titan," *MSNBC*, June 26, 2004, http://www.msnbc.msn.com/id/5294139/.

7. L-3 Communications Titan Group, "Titan Reports Record Quarterly Revenues of $620 Million for the Second Quarter of 2005," July 26, 2005, http://www.titan.com/investor/press-releases/press_releases_display_2005.html?id=32&select=5.

8. Robbins Umeda & Fink, LLP, "Titan, Inc, Securities Fraud Class Action," http://www.ruflaw.com/achievementsi.asp.

9. Willbros, Inc., "About Us," http://www.willbros.com/fw/main/Overview-182.html.

10. Stanford Law School in cooperation with Cornerstone Research, "Willbros, Inc.," *Securities Class Action Clearinghouse*, http://securities.stanford.edu/1034/WG05_01/.

11. BBC News, "Criticism of ditched Saudi probe," *BBC News Online (news.bbc.co.uk)*, December 15, 2006, http://news.bbc.co.uk/2/hi/business/6181977.stm.

12. Cardinal Health, Inc., "Cardinal Health To Acquire Syncor International," June 14, 2002, http://www.cardinal.com/pts/content/news/news0614.asp.

13. *SEC v. Syncor International Corporation* (D.D.C. 2002), Complaint, December 10, 2002, http://www.sec.gov/litigation/complaints/comp17887.htm.

14. U.S. Department of Justice, "Micrus Corporation Enters into Agreement to Resolve Potential Foreign Corrupt Practices Act Liability," March 2, 2005, http://www.usdoj.gov/opa/pr/2005/March/05_crm_090.htm.

15. Ibid.

16. Ibid.

17. U.S. Department of Justice, "DPC (Tianjin) Ltd. Charged with Violating the Foreign Corrupt Practices Act," May 20, 2005, http://www.usdoj.gov/opa/pr/2005/May/05_crm_282.htm.

18. Ibid.

19. SEC Administrative Proceeding in the Matter of Syncor International Corporation, December 10, 2002, File No. 3-10969.

20. U.S. Department of Justice, "DPC (Tianjin) Ltd. Charged with Violating the Foreign Corrupt Practices Act."

21. As reported by the Company in a quarterly filing with the U.S. Securities and Exchange Commission on November 2, 2006.

22. Sarah Boseley, "Drug firms a danger to health – report," *The Guardian*, June 26, 2006.

23. Krysia Diver, "Ratiopharm sales reps in bribe probe," *Associated Press*, December 18, 2006.

24. *World Duty Free Company Ltd v. The Republic of Kenya* (ICSID Case No. ARB/00/7) Award, 4 October 2006, par. 4.

25. Ibid, par. 66.

26. Ibid, par. 188.

27. *United States v. Viktor Kozeny, Frederic Bourke, Jr., and David Pinkerton* (S.D.N.Y. 2005), Indictment.

28. Ibid, 16.

29. U.S. Energy Information Administration, "Equatorial Guinea: Oil," http://www.eia.doe.gov/emeu/cabs/Equatorial_Guinea/Oil.html.

30. Recounted to the author after a TRACE Workshop in Malabo, Equatorial Guinea, February 2006.

31. The ABB Group, "ABB wins $50 million order to strengthen power supply in Mexico," October 30, 2006, http://www.abb.com/cawp/seitp202/04fcc519092e1bc9c12572170030e784.aspx.

32. U.S. Department of Justice, "ABB Vetco Gray, Inc. and ABB Vetco Gray UK Ltd. Plead Guilty to Foreign Bribery Charges," July 6, 2004, http://www.usdoj.gov/criminal/press_room/press_releases/2004_3694_ABB_VETCO_GRAY_INC._AND_ABB_VETCO_GRAY_UK_LTD._PLEAD_GUILTY_TO_FOREIGN_BRIBERY_CHARGES.htm.

33. National Petroleum Investment Management Services, http://www.napims.com/index.html#.

34. U.S. Department of Justice, "ABB Vetco Gray, Inc. and ABB Vetco Gray UK Ltd. Plead Guilty to Foreign Bribery Charges."

35. *SEC v. John Samson, John G. A. Munro, Ian N. Campbell, and John H. Whelan* (D.D.C. 2006); SEC Accounting and Auditing Enforcement Release No. 2456 (July 5, 2006).

36. U.S. Department of Justice, "Three Vetco International Ltd. Subsidiaries Plead Guilty to Foreign Bribery and Agree to Pay $26 Million in Criminal Fines,"

February 6, 2007, http://www.usdoj.gov/opa/pr/2007/February/07_crm_075 .html.

37. The Halliburton joint venture is reportedly under investigation in the United States, the United Kingdom, France, Switzerland and Nigeria. The parties have admitted some of the allegations and continue to dispute others.

38. See the Official Website of Finima, Rivers States, Republic of Nigeria, http://www.finima.org/tour.asp.

39. Katz, "Nigeria bribery case heats up again."

40. Halliburton Company, Form 10-Q Quarterly Report for the period ending September 30, 2006, 58-59.

41. Tesler has confirmed before a French magistrate that he made payments to Jack Stanley. See Hector Igbikiowubo, "TSKJ Saga:Swiss govt freezes $100m accounts," *Vanguard Online*, December 6, 2004, http://news.biafranigeriaworld. com/archive/2004/dec/06/083.html.

42. Halliburton Company, Form 10-Q Quarterly Report for the period ending September 30, 2005, 19.

43. The CIA World Factbook, "Costa Rica," https://www.cia.gov/cia/publications/factbook/geos/cs.html.

44. U.S. Department of Justice, "Former Alcatel CIT Executive is Indicted for Alleged Bribes to Costa Rican Officials to Obtain Mobile Telephone Contract," December 19, 2006, http://www.usdoj.gov/criminal/press_room/press_releases/2006_4898_1_CRM_06-850_fcpa.pdf.

45. *SEC v. John Samson, John G. A. Munro, Ian N. Campbell, and John H. Whelan* (D.D.C. 2006), Complaint, July 5, 2006, http://www.sec.gov/litigation/complaints/2006/comp19754.pdf.

46. Ibid, 6.

47. *SEC v. BellSouth Corporation*, Civ. No. 1:02-CV-0113 (N.D. Ga. 2002); SEC Accounting and Auditing Enforcement Release No. 1494 (Jan. 15, 2002); SEC Administrative Proceeding in the Matter of BellSouth Corporation, January 15, 2002, File No. 3-10678.

48. While in-house counsel with a multinational corporation in the 1990s, the author was asked by a lawyer working on a lawsuit in Indonesia whether his firm was authorized to include "the fees for the judge" in the firm's bill. The firm was advised that it was not so authorized.

49. As of December 2006. See www.bakerhughes.com.

50. SEC Accounting and Auditing Enforcement Release No. 1444 (Sept. 12, 2001); SEC Administrative Proceeding in the Matter of Baker Hughes, September 12, 2001, File No. 3-10572.

51. *Korea Supply Company v. Lockheed Martin Corp.*, Case No. S100136 (Ca. Sup. Ct. 2003); BBC News, "Lockheed sex suit to go ahead," *BBC News Online (news.bbc.co.uk)*, March 5, 2003, http://news.bbc.co.uk/2/hi/business/2820939.stm; Terri Theodore (AP Alert), "U.S. lawsuit alleging bribes, sex favours involving military contract spills into B.C.," *The Canadian Press*, December 1, 2004.

52. Recounted to the author by the intermediary in 2001.

53. Shang-Jin Wei, "Why is Corruption So Much More Taxing Than Tax? Arbitrariness Kills." NBER Working Paper No. 6255 (Cambridge: National Bureau of Economic Research, November 1997).

54. The French National Assembly adopted Law No. 2000-595, the implementation legislation to the OECD Convention on Combating Bribery of Foreign Public Officials in International Business Transactions, on June 30, 2000. Both the implementing legislation and the Convention entered into force on September 29, 2000.

55. John Tagliabue, "French Court Convicts and Jails Ex-Leaders of Oil Company," *New York Times*, November 13, 2003.

56. BBC News, "Total executive in bribery probe," October 20, 2006, http://news.bbc.co.uk/2/hi/business/6068858.stm.

57. For more information on diploma mills, see State of Oregon Student Assistance Commission Office of Degree Authorization, http://www.osac.state.or.us/oda/diploma_mill.html.

58. See *United States v. Richard John Novak*, Case No. CR-05-180-3-LRS (E.D. Wash. March 20, 2006) (Plea Agreement).

59. The Associated Press, "Diploma mill linked to Liberian diplomats," *The Seattle Times*, March 21, 2006, http://seattletimes.nwsource.com/html/localnews/2002879758_webnigerians21.html.

60. AP Alert, "Diploma mill webmaster indicted on child-porn charges," *The Associated Press*, January 26, 2006.

Chapter 6: International Embarrassment

1. This summary of the Oil-for-Food Program and the subsequent investigation draws heavily on the report of the Independent Inquiry Committee led by Paul A. Volcker, which can be found at http://www.iic-offp.org/ and on *Good Intentions Corrupted: The Oil-for-Food Scandal and the Threat to the U.N.*, an informative and highly readable account of the investigation as told by two people who were instrumental to it.

2. Iraqi "leadership" is used here to refer to dictator Saddam Hussein, his relatives and cronies who supported him and benefited from his tyranny, regardless of formal office, whereas Iraqi "government" is used to refer to those holding formal office and the country's civil servants, many of whom lived in fear of the leadership.

3. Adopted by the Security Council on April 3, 1991. The full text is available at the United Nations website: www.un.org/Docs/scres/1991/scres91.htm.

4. Jeffrey A. Meter and Mark G. Califano, *Good Intentions Corrupted: The Oil-for-Food Scandal and the Threat to the U.N.* (New York: PublicAffairs, 2006), xx.

5. The Australian Wheat Board investigation concluded that that entity alone paid about US$220 million in bribes to the Iraqi regime. Not included in these numbers is another US$1.8 billion in revenue that was moved outside the UN escrow account as a part of an extensive oil smuggling scheme involving more than US$11 billion in smuggled oil.

6. CNN News, "Condoleezza Rice To Testify Publicly Before 9/11 Commission, British Police Find Chemical Used for Terror Attacks During Raid, Terror Attack Preempted in The Philippines, Interview with John Edwards - Part 1," *FDCHeMedia Inc.*, March 30, 2004.

7. Independent Inquiry Committee into the United Nations Oil-for-Food Programme, "The Management of the United Nations Oil-for-Food Programme, Volume 1 – The Report of the Committee," September 7, 2005, 45, http://www.iic-offp.org/documents/Sept05/Mgmt_V1.pdf.

8. Ibid, 88.

9. Agence France-Presse, "AWB shrugs off ban from US government contracts, programmes," December 21, 2006.

10. Michael Peel, Haig Simonian and Mark Turner, "Most Iraq oil-for-food scandal perpetrators go unpunished," *Financial Times UK*, December 9, 2006.

11. James Kanter, "Total backs chief on Iraqi oil money," *International Herald Tribune*, October 20, 2006, http://www.iht.com/articles/2006/10/20/business/total.php.

12. In March 2007, de Margerie also was questioned about alleged bribes paid in Iran as a part of the South Pars gas field. See The Associated Press, "Total oil chief in 'bribes' probe."

13. International Olympic Committee, Olympic Charter (Lausanne: International Olympic Committee, August 2004), http://multimedia.olympic.org/pdf/en_report_122.pdf.

14. Philip Hersh, "Marc Hodler: 1918 – 2006, Olympics whistle-blower," *Chicago Tribune*, October 19, 2006.

15. Obituary, "Marc Hodler," *Times (UK)*, October 23, 2006.

16. International Olympics Committee Ethics Commission, "Decision containing Recommendations N° D/01/05, Case N° 1/04," February 4, 2005, http://multimedia.olympic.org/pdf/en_report_913.pdf.

17. John Powers, "Building Speed in Athens it's a Race to the Finish for Games Organizers," *Boston Globe (MA)*, June 13, 2004.

18. Michael Schwirtz, "Arms Exporter Faults U.S. Sanctions," *New York Times*, August 8, 2006.

19. Kerin Hope, Richard Milne and Haig Simonian, "Scandal at Siemens hits joint venture with Nokia," *Financial Times UK*, December 15, 2006.

20. Economist, "Anti-Corruption measures: Too little, too late?" December 16, 2006.

21. Robert J. Saiget (AFP), "More on Beijing Olympic Spokesman Promises Clean Games Despite Scandal," *World News Connection*, June 14, 2006.

22. AP DataStream, "China promises to combat corruption ahead of 2008 Olympics," *The Associated Press*, December 13, 2006.

23. Aaron Benzenbower, "No foul play in gold medal case," *Daily Breeze*, October 31, 2004, A18.

24. Neil Wilson, "Shame of the Bent Judges," *Daily Mail (UK)*, February 20, 2006.

25. Ibid.

26. To date, US$4.6 billion of the US$7.1 billion committed has been delivered.

27. US Federal News, "Tsunami Reconstruction Plan," June 23, 2005.

28. Mel Gunasekera, "Graft costs Sri Lanka a billion dollars a year: whistle-blower," *Agence France-Presse*, January 16, 2007.

29. Western Daily Press, "This corruption is more than major," January 15, 2007.

30. Organisation of Asia Pacific News Agencies, "German Donor Withdraws Humanitarian Aid for Aceh Tsunami Victims," December 20, 2006.

31. See The World Bank website at www.worldbank.org: "About Us – Challenge."

32. The World Bank Group, *Annual Report on Investigations and Sanctions of Staff Misconduct and Fraud and Corruption in Bank-Financed Projects, Fiscal Year 2004* (Washington, DC: The World Bank Group, February 2005), http://siteresources.worldbank.org/INTDOII/Resources/INTFY04Annual-Report2005.pdf.

33. The World Bank, Department of Institutional Integrity, "Fraud and Corruption in Photos," http://go.worldbank.org/1ZEK9VGAR0.

Chapter 7: Preying on the Public

1. The life cycle of bribery really begins before birth. China's "one-child" policy, coupled with the greater cultural value placed on sons, has resulted in the payment of bribes to state doctors to identify and abort baby girls. The bribes induce doctors to participate in the selection process, even though it has been criminalized in China as the country's ratio of boys to girls has become alarmingly unbalanced.

2. This story is described in an article by Celia W. Dugger, "The Hidden Scourge: Taxing the Poor Where a Cuddle With Your Baby Requires a Bribe," *New York Times*, August 30, 2005. The practice also has been confirmed in communications between the author and several women in India.

3. Celia W. Dugger, "The Hidden Scourge: Taxing the Poor Where a Cuddle With Your Baby Requires a Bribe."

4. "China has disclosed that it rescued 3,488 abducted children in 2004, according to the official New China News Agency. Experts say those children are only a fraction of those lost." See Mark Magnier, "Child-Theft Racket Growing in China," *Los Angeles Times*, January 1, 2006.

5. Ibid.

6. Ibid.

7. dpa International Services in English, "Professor sentenced to prison term for helping students cheat," February 16, 2006.

8. South China Morning Post, "Teacher and office worker jailed for exam results scam," January 2, 2006.

9. U.S. State Department, "Training Gives Cambodian Journalists Investigative Skills," State Department Documents, December 1, 2006.

10. Czech Business News, "Czech press review 20/10/2006 – Government & Economy," October 20, 2006.

11. Afghan independent Radio Sahar, "Traffic official arrested taking bribe in west Afghan province," *BBC Monitoring Service (South Asia)*, August 9, 2006.

12. Bernama General News, "Court-Bribe Health Dept Staff Charged With Corruption," October 25, 2004.

13. Peter Hegarty, "City inspector arrested on bribery charges," *Contra Costa Times*, June 27, 2006.

14. EFE Ingles, "Corruption labels don't keep some Brazilians from Congress," October 2, 2006.

15. Lydia Polgreen, "Ivory Coast struggles as ethnic strife spreads," *International Herald Tribune*, November 1, 2005.

16. Interpol, "Trafficking in Human Beings," http://www.interpol.int/Public/THB/default.asp.

17. Human Rights Watch, *HOPES BETRAYED: Trafficking of Women and Girls to Post-Conflict Bosnia and Herzegovina for Forced Prostitution*, vol. 14, no. 9D (November 2002), 28, http://www.hrw.org/reports/2002/bosnia/Bosnia1102-06.htm#P659_121311.

18. Ibid.

19. Human Rights Watch, *Rape for Profit: Trafficking of Nepali Girls and Women to India's Brothels*, vol. 12, no. 5A (October 1995), http://www.hrw.org/reports/1995/India.htm.

20. Holly J. Burkhalter, Vice President, International Justice Mission, Testimony before the Committee on the Judiciary's Subcommittee on Human Rights, U.S. Senate, March 26, 2007, http://judiciary.senate.gov/testimony.cfm?id=2613&wit_id=6204.

21. Human Rights Watch, *HOPES BETRAYED: Trafficking of Women and Girls to Post-Conflict Bosnia and Herzegovina for Forced Prostitution*, 32-33.

22. Holly J. Burkhalter, Vice President, International Justice Mission, Testimony before the Committee on the Judiciary's Subcommittee on Human Rights, U.S. Senate, March 26, 2007.

23. Hindu (India), "Police Officer Suspended," *Financial Times Ltd.*, November 4, 2005.

24. Ibid.

25. Polly Hui and Stefanie Leung, "Health Officials admit bodies pile up; Families receive apology over mortuary outrage," *South China Morning Post*, July 7, 2005.

26. Recounted to the author by the Vice President of a U.S. pharmaceutical company, November 2004.

27. World Food Programme, "Introduction," http://www.wfp.org/aboutwfp/introduction/hunger_fight.asp?section=1&sub_section=1.

28. World Food Programme, "Mission," http://www.wfp.org/aboutwfp/mission/index.asp?section=1&sub_section=6.

29. Save the Children UK, "From Camp to Community: Liberia study on exploitation of children," Discussion Paper, 2006, http://www.savethechildren.org/publications/liberia-exploitation-v4.pdf.

30. Ibid, 14.

31. Ibid, 11.

32. World Food Programme, "HIV/AIDS & Children: Bringing Hope to a Generation," June 2006, 1.

33. Save the Children UK, "From Camp to Community: Liberia study on exploitation of children," 12.

34. Candidate for UN Secretary General, Ashraf Ghani, stated that, "Only by establishing trust in the organization can we make the United Nations the instrument of global choice for addressing the problems of our time." In Ashraf Ghani, "Why I Should Run the U.N.; Climate of Distrust," *The New York Times*, sec. A, September 28, 2006.

35. FDCH Capital Transcripts, "Stephane Dujarric Holds Office Of The Spokesman For The U.N. Secretary General Regular News Briefing," May 8, 2006.

36. Soutik Biswas, "Vajpayee demands murder inquiry," *BBC News Online (news.bbc.co.uk)*, December 10, 2003, http://news.bbc.co.uk/1/hi/world/south_asia/3306075.stm.

37. Amitav Ranjan, "Whistleblower said don't name me. Govt did. He was shot dead," *The Sunday Express*, November 30, 2003, http://www.indianexpress .com/full_story.php?content_id=36329.

38. BBC News, "Suicides in Indian murder case," *BBC News Online (news .bbc.co.uk)*, February 2, 2004, http://news.bbc.co.uk/2/hi/south_asia/3451537 .stm.

Chapter 8: Mounting Impatience

1. September 17, 2006 plenary session, "Partnerships to Combat Corruption: Rising to the Challenge," at the Program of Seminars of the 2006 International Monetary Fund/World Bank Group/Board of Governors Annual Meetings held September 16-18, 2006 in Singapore, http://web.worldbank.org/WBSITE/ EXTERNAL/NEWS/0,,contentMDK:21070091~menuPK:34476~pagePK:34370 ~piPK:34424~theSitePK:4607,00.html.

2. The Lesotho case study upon which this chapter is based was first presented by Professor Stephen Wrage at a Central European International Studies Association conference in Budapest on June 27, 2003.

3. The term "wage earners" does not include the 86% of the population that doesn't earn wages, but rather engages in subsistence agriculture. Of those who fall into the wage earner category, 40% work in South Africa and another 45% in fact are unemployed. The largest and fastest growing employer of wage earners within Lesotho is the garment assembly trade which lately has benefited from foreign direct investment from Taiwan.

4. The CIA World Factbook, "Lesotho," https://www.cia.gov/cia/publications/factbook/geos/lt.html. Lesotho provides a GNP per capita figure of about US$550 per year that is spectacularly low, and yet it disguises the true burden of poverty bourne by the people of Lesotho. Only a handful of countries on earth have a greater disparity of income between the richest few and the abysmally poor many. The wealthiest tenth of the population enjoys almost half the national income while the poorer half possess only about a tenth of the national wealth. The United Nations ranks Lesotho one step above Myanmar (the former Burma) on its Human Development Index.

5. Gregg Easterbrook, writing in *The New Republic* (July 29, 2002), notes that "the anti-globalization movement... has successfully mau-maued all the World Bank and other donor institutions into withdrawing essentially all support for the construction of hydro-dams..." But in this case the World Bank led the initial funding effort with US$8 million in subsidized loans to finance the design of the project and the search for governmental lenders and commercial investors. It also granted US$110 million for the initial phase of construction. The Development Bank of South Africa, the African Development Bank, the European Development Fund and the export credit agencies of a number of European countries were significant contributors. A number of European commercial banks extended loans, but the largest investor was the government of South Africa which paid over US$2.5 billion for the tunnels to bear the water from the dams to the plains. Lesotho committed to raise US$23 million for a hydroelectric station at the Muela dam but construction of this portion was delayed.

6. "Oakville Engineering Company Braces for African Bribery Verdict," *Toronto Star*, September 12, 2002, D11. Water royalties earned from South Africa amounted to about 2.5% of Lesotho's GDP. *Africa News*, January 24, 2003.

7. L. F. Maema, KC, Attorney General of Lesotho, remarks at the 11th International Anti-Corruption Conference, Seoul, 25-28 May 2003, "Prosecuting Bribery in Lesotho," http://admin.corisweb.org/index.php?fuseaction=resource. view&id=111298&src=pub.

8. A detailed account of the trials has been written by Fiona Darroch, Barrister, Grays Inn, London: The Lesotho Corruption Trials: A Case Study, http://admin. corisweb.org/files/Darroch2003_lesotho_courruption_trials1125324795.pdf.

9. Switzerland's implementing legislation to the OECD Convention on Combating Bribery of Foreign Public Officials in International Business Transactions is the Law of 22 December 1999 amending the Swiss Penal Code.

10. L. F. Maema, KC, Attorney General of Lesotho, remarks at the 11th International Anti-Corruption Conference, Seoul, 25-28 May 2003, "Prosecuting Bribery in Lesotho." Mr. Guido Penzhorn, lead counsel on behalf of the Lesotho government in the Sole case, described the same meeting in a presentation before the Committee on Development and Cooperation of the European Parliament on June 12, 2003. (Copy of the presentation supplied to the author by Mr. Penzhorn.) "Mention is made here of a meeting in Pretoria, South Africa, in November 1999, attended by the writer [Mr. Penzhorn], where the EU representative is recorded in the official minutes as expressing 'a willingness. . . to contribute to the cost of the process [the current prosecutions] through their regular assistance programme if they received a request.' The British High Commissioner for Lesotho in turn stated 'that DFID [Department of International Development] could possibly offer direct assistance, even though a part of the EU.'"

11. Callisto and Sarbib, "Corruption and The World Bank (Cont'd)," *The Washington Post*, September 12, 1999.

12. The charge sheet included the following companies, their home countries, and the sums they were alleged to have paid Mr. Sole: ABB, Sweden, US$40,410; Impregilo, Italy, US$250,000; Sogreah, France, US$13,578; Lahmeyer International, Germany, US$8,674; Highlands Water Venture (consortium including Impregilo, Hochtief (Germany), Bouygues (France), Keir International (UK), Sterling International (UK), Concor (South Africa) and Group Five (South Africa), US$733,404; Lesotho Highlands Project Contractors (consortium including Balfour Beatty (UK), Spie Batignolles (France), et alia) US$57,269; Acres International, Canada, US$185,002; Spie Batignolles, France, US$119,393; Dumez International, Nigeria and France, US$82,422; ED Zublin, Germany, US$444,466; Diwi Consulting, Germany, US$2,439; LHPC Chantiers (international consortium), US$63,959.

13. "Lesotho: Africa's Best Kept Secret," *The New African*, May 1, 2003.

14. See Nicol Degli Innocenti, "Lesotho Highlands Bribes Trial Starts," *London Financial Times*, June 5, 2000.

15. L. F. Maema, KC, Attorney General of Lesotho, remarks at the 11th International Anti-Corruption Conference, Seoul, 25-28 May 2003, "Prosecuting Bribery in Lesotho."

16. Ibid. See also Penzhorn's presentation to the European Parliament Committee on Development and Co-Operation. A spokesperson for the World Bank

has said that Lesotho had been offered technical assistance, but that while the Bank could fund "capacity-building" of judicial systems, "we stop short of funding individual cases." See statement by Caroline Anstey of the World Bank quoted in Business Ethics Direct, published by the Ethics Institute of South Africa on their web site at www.ethicsa.com/BED_art_LesothoLHDA. html, accessed 16 July 2003.

17. In an April 2003 judgment passed down by The Appeal Court of Lesotho, the three judges observed Mr. Sole's silence and would not speculate on its significance, except to note that "some payments to the appellant were made by consultants after his dismissal from the Lesotho Highlands Development Agency. This does not detract from our conclusions. The evidence clearly showed that the appellant remained influential in the LHDA long after he left. There may also have been other reasons for these later payments but it is not necessary to speculate on these." In the matter between Ephraim Masupha Sole and The Crown, Court of Appeals (CRI) 5 of 2002, 31.

18. Quoted in *Insight in the News*, October 15, 2002.

19. It was not until 2006 that the Bank debarred a multinational corporation. Prior to then, an examination of the list posted on the Bank's web site would have revealed that roughly a third of the entities on the list were based in Indonesia and a majority were either individuals or very small companies. There were no major corporations on the list. With regard to Acres International, Mr. George Soteroff, a public relations specialist employed by Acres and based in Toronto, argued that "The evidence that was before the World Bank debarment hearing was the same material evidence that the Lesotho prosecutor had, so there is no new material evidence that Acres is aware of." Mr. Soteroff overlooked the point that the prosecutor made available to all who read the trial transcript compelling evidence in the form of formerly secret Swiss bank records. He also overlooked the fact that the World Bank Sanctions Committee is to draw its conclusions based on "the preponderance of evidence," a far lower standard than the criminal court's "beyond a reasonable doubt." The criminal court was able to reach a conviction while the World Bank sustained its earlier blanket finding.

20. According to a World Bank press release, "the period of ineligibility may be reduced by four years if the Bank determines that Lahmeyer has met specific compliance conditions and fully cooperated with the Bank in disclosing past sanctionable misconduct." See "World Bank Sanctions Lahmeyer International for Corrupt Activities in Bank-Financed Projects," November 6, 2006, http://web.worldbank.org/WBSITE/EXTERNAL/NEWS/0,,contentMDK:21116129~menuPK:51062078~pagePK:34370~piPK:34424~theSitePK:4607,00.html.

21. Financial Mail (South Africa), "Another Week," *Financial Times Ltd.*, March 5, 2004.

22. John Saunders, "German firm faces possible blacklisting," *The Globe and Mail*, April 13, 2004.

23. Razina Munshi, "Getting Away With Graft in Africa," *AllAfrica.com*, July 7, 2005. See also Chantelle Benjamin, "SA To Help Lesotho Sue Corrupt Contractors," *Business Day (South Africa)*, March 18, 2004, ". . .the Lesotho Appeal upheld the conviction of companies belonging to a consortium, including SA companies Concor and Group Five; British companies Keir International and Stirling International; and a German company Hochtief for paying

Lesotho Highlands Development Authority head, Masupha Sole, a bribe of [US]$375,000."

24. Chantelle Benjamin, "SA To Help Lesotho Sue Corrupt Contractors."

25. The World Bank, "World Bank Sanctions Lahmeyer International for Corrupt Activities in Bank-Financed Projects."

26. L. F. Maema, KC, Attorney General of Lesotho, remarks at the 11th International Anti-Corruption Conference, Seoul, 25-28 May 2003, "Prosecuting Bribery in Lesotho."

27. All of the international conventions discussed require countries to have or implement national laws that pull the conventions' provisions down into domestic law. The conventions have no automatic effect. As such, technically, a country can have ratified multiple international conventions without ever criminalizing the behavior the conventions are designed to deter.

28. Thirty-four member states are signatories to the OAS Convention. Barbados is the only signatory that has not ratified. The thirty-four states do not include Cuba; while Cuba remains an OAS member, its government has been excluded from participation since 1962.

29. Private-to-private bribery would include the payment of a bribe by an office supply company to the office manager of, for example, a law firm in exchange for an arrangement to purchase its office supplies from the former. While this may skew market forces and certainly results in the office manager enriching himself without regard to the law firm's best interests, it does not involve the abuse of public office and public trust described elsewhere in this book.

Conclusion: Modest Optimism

1. Ethan A. Nadelmann, "Global Prohibition Regimes: The Evolution of Norms in International Society." *International Organization* 44, no. 4 (Autumn, 1990), 479-526.

2. The Crédit Mobilier scandal of the late 1860s implicated President Garfield and more than a dozen congressmen in a corrupt deal orchestrated by construction company Crédit Mobilier.

3. On the bringing of order to unregulated territories, see Debra L. Spar, *Ruling the Waves: Cycles of Discovery, Chaos and Wealth from the Compass to the Internet* (New York: Harcourt, 2001).

4. Adam Hochschild, *Bury the Chains: Prophets and Rebels in the Fight to Free and Empire's Slaves* (Boston: Houghton Mifflin, 2005), 67.

5. United Nations, "United Nations Convention Against Corruption," October 31, 2003, Article 46.

6. United Nations, "United Nations Convention Against Corruption," October 31, 2003, Article 48.

7. Jimmy Burns and James Boxell, "US protested at axing of BAE probe," *Financial Times*, April 26, 2007.

8. Jonathan Rauch, "Seeing Around Corners," *The Atlantic Monthly*, April 2002.

9. Most European countries provided for tax deductions for bribes as business expenses prior to the adoption of the OECD Convention.

10. Agence France-Presse, "No holiday 'red envelope' bribery for officials in southern China."

11. Ibid.

12. The return of funds was delayed in part by concerns that the money would not be managed for the good of the Nigerian people once returned. Ultimately, the Nigeria and Swiss governments agreed to ground rules addressing how the money would be spent and both parties agreed that the World Bank would play a role in oversight of the expenditures.

13. Agence France-Presse, "Philippines To Consider Offer From Marcos Over Allegedly Embezzled Assets," May 4, 2006.

14. Ibid. According to the AFP report: "Ricardo Abcede, a senior official with the Presidential Commission on Good Government (PCGG), said he had held "exploratory talks" with Marcos ' lawyer Robert Sison. Abcede said both agreed to come up with a draft agreement on the stolen wealth."

15. Ibid.

16. AP Alert, "Swiss urge other countries to speed return of dictator cash," *The Associated Press*, October 3, 2006.

17. Annie I. Bang, "Prosecutors Probe Chun Slush Fund," *The Korea Herald*, November 14, 2006.

18. Schabir Shaik's conviction was upheld on appeal on November 7, 2006.

19. Joe Humphreys, "Court decision may hit Zuma's career," *The Irish Times*, sec. World, November 7, 2006.

20. Ibid.

21. The Houston Chronicle, "In Brief: Chinese official put to death for bribes," February 15, 2004, A24.

22. Ibid.

23. Calum MacLeod, "China plans to use death penalty more sparingly," *USA TODAY*, sec. News, May 16, 2006.

24. Editorial, "Not Easy for DPP To Put Distance Between Party, Taiwan's First Family," *Taipei Times*, November 12, 2006, 8.

25. Asian Political News, "2ND LD: KMT grabs Taipei, DPP gets Kaohsiung in Taiwan mayoral elections," *Kyodo News International, Inc.*, December 11, 2006.

26. The Associated Press, "AP Poll: Lawmaker standing falls among public," *MSNBC*, December 8, 2005, http://www.msnbc.msn.com/id/10387184/.

27. Matangi Tonga Online, "Judge favours fine over imprisonment due to Veikune's heart condition," *Vava'u Press Ltd.*, February 16, 2006, http://www.matangitonga.to/scripts/artman/exec/view.cgi?archive=5&num=1631.

28. Kevin Bohn and Terry Frieden, "Affidavit: $90,000 found in Congressman's freezer," *CNN.com*, May 22, 2006. http://www.cnn.com/2006/POLITICS/05/21/jefferson.search/index.html.

29. AP Online, "Swiss lawyer returns home after deportation to U.S. on suspicion of money laundering," *The Associated Press*, November 2, 2004.

30. Ibid.

31. *United States v. Kay*, 359 F3d 738 (5th Cir. 2004).

32. American Rice, acquired by Spanish food company SOS Cuetara in 2003, was not a part of the lawsuit.

33. See *United States v. Richard John Novak*, Case No. CR-05-180-3-LRS (E.D. Wash. March 20, 2006) (Plea Agreement).

34. See *United States v. Head*, Case No. 06-CR1380-BEN (S.D. Cal. June 23, 2006) (Plea Agreement).

35. At every TRACE Workshop held to date, one or more executives have asked about the nexus between bribery by corporations and personal culpability on the part of management.

36. Richard Milne, "Siemens bribery scandal raises further questions," *Financial Times UK*, December 22, 2006.

37. John Goff, "Coming Distractions: If these eight risks are not on your radar screen, they will be soon," *CFO Magazine*, April 1, 2006.

38. Kate Burgess, "Corruption creeps into investors' consciences. . ." *Financial Times*, December 23, 2006.

39. Ibid.

40. Editorial, "New in the 'bu," *Los Angeles Times*, November 19, 2006.

Selected Bibliography

Abed, George T., and Sanjeev Gupta, eds. *Governance, Corruption & Economic Performance*. Washington, DC: International Monetary Fund, 2002.

Deming, Stuart H. *The Foreign Corrupt Practices Act and the New International Norms*. Chicago: The American Bar Association, 2005.

Elliot, Kimberly Ann, ed. *Corruption and the Global Economy*. Washington, DC: Institute of International Economics, 1997.

Jain, Arvind K., ed. *Economics of Corruption*. Boston: Kluwer Academic Publishers, 1998.

Kaufmann, Daniel, and Shan-Jin Wei. "Does 'Grease Money' Speed up the Wheels of Commerce?" Paper presented at the American Economic Association Meeting, Chicago, IL, 1998.

Klitgaard, Robert. *Controlling Corruption*. Berkeley: University of California Press, 1988.

———. *Tropical Gangsters*. New York: Basic Books, 1990.

Mauro, Paolo. "Corruption and Growth." *Quarterly Journal of Economics* 110, no. 3 (August 1995): 681–712.

Mauss, Marcel. *The Gift: The Form and Reason for Exchange in Archaic Societies*. Translated by W.D. Halls. London: Routledge, 1990. Originally published as *Essai sur le Don* (Paris: Presses Universitaires de France, 1950).

Meyer, Jeffrey A. and Mark G. Califano. *Good Intentions Corrupted: The Oil-for-Food Scandal and the Threat to the U.N.* New York: PublicAffairs, 2006.

Naím, Moisés. "The Corruption Eruption." *Brown Journal of World Affairs* 2, no. 2 (Summer 1995): 245–61.

Noonan, John T. Jr. *Bribes*. New York: Macmillan, 1984.

Organisation for Economic Cooperation and Development. "Convention on Combating Bribery of Foreign Public Officials in International Business Transactions." November 21, 1997.

Organization of American States. "Inter-American Convention against Corruption." March 29, 1996.

Rose-Ackerman, Susan. *Corruption and Government: Causes, Consequences, and Reform*. Cambridge: Cambridge University Press, 1999.

Smarzynska, Beata K., and Shang-Jin Wei. "Corruption and the Composition of Foreign Direct Investment: Firm-Level Evidence." Policy Research Working Paper WPS 2360 (Washington, DC: World Bank, 2000).

Theobold, Robin. *Corruption, Development and Underdevelopment*. Durham: Duke University Press, 1990.

United Nations. "United Nations Convention Against Corruption." October 31, 2003.

United States. *The Foreign Corrupt Practices Act, U.S. Code* 15, § 78dd–1 et seq.

———. *The Hobbs Act, U.S. Code* 18, § 1951.

Wei, Shang-Jin. "Why is Corruption So Much More Taxing Than Tax? Arbitrariness Kills." NBER Working Paper No. 6255 (Cambridge: National Bureau of Economic Research, November 1997).

Index

About the Author

ALEXANDRA ADDISON WRAGE is an international attorney and President of TRACE International, a non-profit anti-bribery business association with over 1,000 corporate members in more than 100 countries. She has worked as in-house counsel for both Northrop Grumman Corporation and MCI Communications. She has written numerous articles on practical anti-bribery strategies and speaks frequently on topics of international law and the hidden costs of corruption. A Canadian, Wrage studied law at Kings College, Cambridge University, and lives now in Annapolis, Maryland.

CPSIA information can be obtained at www.ICGtesting.com
Printed in the USA
BVOW012331230513

321342BV00002B/2/P